From Every Chink of the Ark

By Peter Redgrove

The Collector and Other Poems
Routledge & Kegan Paul

The Nature of Cold Weather and Other Poems
Routledge & Kegan Paul

At the White Monument and Other Poems
Routledge & Kegan Paul

The Force and Other Poems
Routledge & Kegan Paul

Work in Progress (Poems 1969)
Poet & Printer Press

The Hermaphrodite Album (with Penelope Shuttle)
Fuller D'Arch Smith

Dr Faust's Sea-Spiral Spirit and Other Poems
Routledge & Kegan Paul

In the Country of the Skin
Routledge & Kegan Paul

The Terrors of Dr Treviles (with Penelope Shuttle)
Routledge & Kegan Paul

Sons of my Skin (Selected Poems 1954 - 1974)
(chosen and introduced by Marie Peel)
Routledge & Kegan Paul

The Glass Cottage (with Penelope Shuttle)
Routledge & Kegan Paul

Miss Carstairs Dressed For Blooding
and Other Plays
Marion Boyars

From Every Chink of the Ark

AND OTHER NEW POEMS

by

PETER REDGROVE

Routledge & Kegan Paul
London, Henley and Boston

First published in 1977
by Routledge & Kegan Paul Ltd
39 Store Street,
London WC1E 7DD,
Reading Road,
Henley-on-Thames,
Oxon RG9 1EN and
9 Park Street,
Boston, Mass. 02108, USA
Printed in Great Britain by
Lowe & Brydone Ltd

British Library Cataloguing in Publication Data

Redgrove, Peter.
From Every Chink of the Ark.
I. Title
821'.9'14   PR6035.E267F/

ISBN 0-7100-8531-1

Contents

Acknowledgments

Grateful acknowledgments are due to the following magazines and anthologies in which certain of the poems first appeared:

Anteus, Best SF 1976, Closedown Sequence (BBC2 TV), *Delta, Encounter, Gallery, Gallimaufry, The Hudson Review, Littack, The Little Word Machine, The London Magazine, Malenka, Matrix, Meridian, New Headland, New Humanist, New Poems 1975-6, New Poems 1976-7* (PEN), *New Poetry I, New Poetry II,* (Arts Council), *New Statesman, Orbis, Pink Peace, Poems for Shakespeare 1973, Poetry Dimension 3, Poetry in the 70s, Poetry Now* (BBC), *Poetry Review, Prospice, Sceptre Press Pamphlets, The Scotsman, 2nd Aeon, Stand, The Times Literary Supplement, Westward Look* (BBC), *Words Broadsheets,* The Whitechapel Gallery City of London Exhibition.

Some of the poems appeared in individual BBC programmes, to which acknowledgment is also given: *Drama Now* ('Dance the Putrefact'); *The God of Glass* ('White Lady Falls'); *The Little Professor* ('Yoga Ogre', 'Dog Prospectus', 'Sleep of the Great Hypnotist', 'Serious Readers', 'The Barbers'.) 'My Shirt of Small Checks' was featured in *The Best of Poetry Now.*

He Is

He is a Green Man in a full suit of fruit,
He is the voice of that tree, he is
An icy shiver from a spiral draught, he is
The seven metals shelf-arranged, he is
A buzz in the air and a cough in the silk
He is a groan deep in the privet,
On the road he is a grinning dog
With one black eyelid and one white
Who commits his act of light
With a ginger bitch,
Large sweet soul.

He is a god who breathes applebreath
Like an orchard of cider,
Breathing like a baby, without expectation,
Like a wheatfield, like a waterfall.
He brings the lamps
Through the waterfall, through the wheatfield.

Dog Prospectus

The dog must see your corpse. The last thing that
  you feel
Must be the dog's warm-tufa licking of your hand,
Its clear gaze on your trembling lips, then
Snapping at flies, catches the last breath in its teeth,
And trots off with you quickly to the Judge,
Your advocate and friend. The corpse a dog has not
  seen
Pollutes a thousand men; the Bishop's hound
Tucked like a cushion at his tombstone feet
Once through the door carries a helix staff
And looks like Hermes on that side, the Bishop
  tumbling
On the puppy-paws of death...
                         as a temporary Professor
  at this U
I practice, when the campus swarms with them,
Focusing out the students, so the place
Is amply empty, except for a few dogs.
They should study here, the U enrol them
And take more fees, at agreed standards teaching
Elementary Urinology, and Advanced
Arboreal Urinology: The Seasons and their Smells;
Freshman Osteology: The Selection and Concealment
Of Bones; Janissology: The Budding Watchdog, with
Fawning, a two-semester course. Lunar
  Vocalisation,

Or Baying at the Moon; the 'lame-dog bid for
   sympathy
With big sad eyes and hanging tongue,' which is
Cosmetic Opthalmology with Intermittent
   Claudication
In the Rhetorical Physiognomy Gym. Shit and Its
   Meaning;
Coprology: the Dog-Turd and Modern Legislation;
   The
Eating of Jezebel, or Abreactive Phantasising; The
   Black Dog,
Or Studies in Melancholy; The Age of Worry
An Era Favorable to Dogs... ...
                              How to Beg:
A Long-Term Economic Good; with How to Fuck,
Or Staggering in Six-Legged Joy; Fleas,
A Useful Oracle and in this same last year
The Dedicated Castrate or God's Eunuch,
The Canine Celibate as Almost-Man;
And finally how, if uncastrated,
To change places and become Master-Dog,
The Palindromic Homocane and Goddog-Doggod,
Wise Hermes of the Intelligent Nose

Leading to the Degree of Master of Hounds.

The campus throngs with hounds, this degree
Is very popular, alas,
I focus them out: in ample emptiness
A few humans hurry to their deep study
Without prospectus, without University.
This one is desirous of becoming a perfect scribe:
He knows vigilance, ferocity, and how to bark;
This one studies gazing as the dogs used to
On the images of the gods, as prophets should.
What gods, what images?

Those glorious trees, trilling with birds, cicadas,
Pillars of the sky, our books and ancestors;
I piss my tribute here, I cannot help it;
The few humans left, noble as dogs once were,
Piss on this university.

Yoga Voyage

The yogin is an anti-crank, a kind of on-board
   gymnast.
He scoffs at religion as he twines his limbs.
While Master unwinds to a disc of Tchaikowsky
I pick my nose during this yoga-lecture
Which is mere P.T.;
I have more interest in this than that,
This too is a yoga, call it reverie,
Call it *nosah-yogah;*
I am a bogi-yogi.

As our voyage unwinds
The serious frowns fade from the polished spoons,
The mouth lights up with freshest breakfast-eggs
From the ship's batteries, the salt water breezes.
Our prows feel pointed and our bright-work gleams.
Each sports a liner in his voyaging trousers,
The women watch the dark sea with great eyes like
   portholes;
Call it *linah-yogah.*

All is provided: the Chief Engineer
Will hear confessions in the Cinema
From six till dinner-gong; we are guests
In a mansion full of spinning shafts
Shining with greasy glory, and furnace fires
Blazing unseen in dogged steel cabinets.
All night we dash to the U.S. like a water-train,
Like a tattered golden moth blown through the
    darkness,
Joints pouring light, and every
Screwed-down panel creaks a different note,
Squeaking comfortably like a seven-league boot.
Call it *ogre-yogah.*

In the mornings, water-gongs; the sea so blue
In sunshine it falls to liquid ashes, grey,
You need your polaroids, while the dark passage-
    pulses
Hypnotically reverse the small waves' sense:
The troughs seem tall and the bright crests deep.
Small shocks of seaweed spread about
Orange as tobacco. Night brings in
A polished silver chocolate-pot with deep reflections
And neat white envelopes with the Captain's summons.
Dingy as used tissues, steam is snatched away
By the wind that crumples England, call it
Departurah-yogah, aurevwa-yogah.

The Breathing-Place

I.

The breathing-place. A sadness at the root,
At the root of it that leaves him weepy.
Touch me there, he says, it is my sadness.
Your picture in each falling raindrop
Your hair blowing as the rain falls
Your hair in the waters as they unfold
Your hair brushing me as you read me
Does not compensate. Touch me there, he says,
At my root, in that spot, my sadness.

II.
Well, what do you expect, she says, it is salt,
There is a finer lustre, what do you expect?
The cohabitation of saints? The halo'd penis?
The stiff charged wire spitting magnetism?
There is not a single mirror in the saints' house
Yet it seems full of mirrors as they make their love
Splashed everywhere like the white facsimiles of salt,
Like white flies, or mass-production shirts.
This gesture of his, caught by her, both laughing,
Leaning back, and the infinity of arms!
The rain falls with their faces on it,
They are endless statues of themselves on the
    chimney-breasts,
They dance numerously as grass-blades on the lanky
    lawn,
They fume incense of themselves, their tiny
Bronze nails clash, the tamboura whines OM as they
    bare their teeth,
The house is infested with the lovers, no one could
    live there again,
The pungent dust is made of them, the great garden-
    tree
Plunging roots from its branches is he and she!
Intolerable! They are never sad. Touch me
Here, she says, at my root, in that sadness.

From Every
Chink of the Ark

We are all still because the sea is moving so hard.
We are turtleshells carved with the heads of eagles,
We are tiny black unbreathing gibbon-nipples,
We are a clenched tapestry of eels
And two arid scorpions brooching our boulder,
And two goody-grabbing blowflies like muddy studs.
We are lizards that freeze becoming marble
    icecreams
We are iguanas that empty themselves out of
    enamelled tennis-shoes,
We are a python that is a bough with tightly-shut lids
In a green fruit still as our sloughed skin
Which is a glass canoe full of scurf.

The squid is breathing jewels, he is amethyst
In pulses no tourmaline yes chrysolite;
The lion in fact paces, but as syrup paces.

We are not what we seem the bats are only macintosh
Captain Noah and his seven are boxwood, he is
    Captain Nemo
They are also suits of armour marked vacant not for
    drowning
While the poison waters collide like green ghosttrains
One immense fruity corpsecake slicing itself instantly

9

We are not offensive we are a lean smile on stilts
Greyhounds of broomstick, alligators of icon,
Leopards of netsuke, soothing-stone snails

But water bustles and brays
Like a great green ass rolling in white thistles

Our ass is a gold statue, ready to topple,
Be brayed in water, and drunk
Fate's football

The footballers are furious
Striped currents
The referee is whistling his winds
The sky is a face-stadium
Spit-angry with millions

The interior of the football
Quiet as the Vatican in wartime
Nothing stirs, hugging itself

Ararat's peak
Nothing stirs

Then from every chink
A new world!

The boat blows away.

Tapestry Moths

(For Vicky Allen)

I know a curious moth, that haunts old buildings,
A tapestry moth, I saw it at Hardwick Hall,
'More glass than wall' full of great tapestries
  laddering
And bleaching in the white light from long windows.
I saw this moth when inspecting one of the cloth
  pictures
Of a man offering a basket of fresh fruit through a
  portal
To a ghost with other baskets of lobsters and
  pheasants nearby
When I was amazed to see some plumage of one of
  the birds
Suddenly quiver and fly out of the basket
Leaving a bald patch on the tapestry, breaking up as
  it flew away.
A claw shifted. The ghost's nose escaped. I realised

It was the tapestry moths that ate the colours like
    the light
Limping over the hangings, voracious cameras,
And reproduced across their wings the great scenes
    they consumed
Carrying the conceptions of artists away to hang in
    the woods
Or carried off never to be joined again or packed
    into microscopic eggs
Or to flutter like fragments of old arguments through
    the unused kitchens
Settling on pans and wishing they could eat the
    glowing copper

The lamb-faced moth with shining amber wool dust-
    dabbing the pane
Flocks of them shirted with tiny fleece and picture
    wings
The same humble mask flaming in the candle or on
    the glass bulb
Scorched unwinking, dust-puff, disassembled; a
    sudden flash among the hangings
Like a window catching the sun, it is a flock of moths
    golden from eating
The gold braid of the dress uniforms, it is the rank
    of the family's admirals
Taking wing, they rise

Out of horny amphorae, pliable maggots, wingless
    they champ
The meadows of fresh salad, the green glowing
    pilasters
Set with flowing pipes and lines like circuits in green
    jelly
Later they set in blind moulds all whelked and horny
While the moth-soup inside makes itself lamb-faced
    in
The inner theatre with its fringed curtains, the long-
    dressed
Moth with new blank wings struggling over tapestry,
    drenched with its own birth juices

Tapestry enters the owls, the pipistrelles, winged
    tapestry
That flies from the Hall in the night to the street
    lamps,
The great unpicturing wings of the nightfeeders on
    moths
Mute their white cinders... and a man,
Selecting a melon from his mellow garden under a
    far hill, eats,
Wakes in the night to a dream of one offering fresh
    fruit,
Lobsters and pheasants through a green fluted portal
    to a ghost.

The Sleep
of the Great Hypnotist

The sleep of the great hypnotist, who is underground,
Who is hypnotised on his monument with his stone
    book,
Who on his death-bed gave her a trance and into that
    openness
Dropped his posthumous suggestion, and died
As she awoke. Now she will never be free of him,
And it is night, and all the water speaks in his voice
Out of the springs under the pine-belts haunted by
    tawny ghosts,
(Great cheated hypnotists, the red owners of the
    land,)
And now he with his spirit command has opened up
    this land to her,
Her decent campus alive with the indecently dead,
    her father
Somewhere among them who has told her to dream of
    him and shed
Spirit tears. The Indian Museum commands her to it
Where there are nose-bones, and painted sticks for
    the hair,
Effigy-pipes that are portable altars with a spirit to
    consult
That blows gentle blue whirlwinds from his carved-
    open head,
And there are skulls stained green from brass
    kettles in the soil,

And there are reindeer combs for causing dreams,
Cootie-combs to comb dreams into your hair before
  you sleep,
Gesumaria combs to comb fine orgasms into your
  hair;
And the dead Hypnotist's command unlocks this case
  with her hand
And visions of running horses pass through her head
As his orders pass the comb through her mane...

Among all these Indians and knowledge where is her
  father,
Where, in this newly-alive world full of the dead?
A woman whose oily plaits shine in the starlight
  smiles at her:
"He is not born yet," and pats her global tummy;

So she dreams of the great hypnotist among the
  Indian relics
By post-hypnosis after his death, and in the
  graveyard
The dead man tries to turn over one more page in
  his cold stone book.

Over the dark snow, somebody throws a great
  window-spark open

His last experiment wishes she were that squaw.

The Stains

The woman in the besmutched dress
It was I who was afraid and the Indians rising
The powder from those muskets   the puffs
Of smoke from our own cannon were harmless
But the smoke stained my sleeves   thus I drifted
Like an off-white truce   a half-hearted white flag
In my stained blouse with the high neck
And bosom-tucks and little fringes, my
Satin skirt with the waterfall back
My long stained skirt that made me glide
Stained with the muddy ground and gunsmoke
This orderly was helping me escape
My husband was busy with the war
I went in a besmutched dress across the frontier
Like a butcher's wife between the staining cannon
Between the groaning men   I saw my husband
In his red uniform lacquered in its colour
I saw his head shatter in a plume
Of coloured smoke that stained me
I cradled it, in my spattered skirt
I crossed the frontier into night and safety
There was a smoking train whose smoke stained
I sat besmattered with the train
Besmattered with the cattle-leavings in the train
A dog sniffed at my dress

As though it were a map of battles and escape
My history written for him in my dress
The dog sniffed at my dress like my child
His thorny pads tick-tocked away from me
The train lurched, new firing began to spatter me.

Pictures from a Shirtmaker's Apprentice

I.
The palaces he rebuilds by changing his shirt!
Tying new ties: not decoration at all,
But navigation! it is the mystic weave
Of fingers, the prestidigital passes
Over magic sheens, the game with one's throat
Dressed and undressed in pyramids and bands.
One knots his tie, wedges between starched points
The intrinsicate cravat, and enters his car
With portentous briefcase, gripping the wheel:
He would as soon drive collarless as release his
    hands.
The stiff neck, well-guarded, repels all ghosts.
But at home the tie comes off, and welcome ghosts!
As the shirt opens, it blouses with warm airs;
The mystic triangle at the throat, he sees with
    qualms,
Matches his wife's...

I sex shirts and design men's ties, which is to say
I design the thoughts you have about each other
Sitting at tables in restaurants and boardrooms
Speaking your words from throats I dress.
May I flay you a red to wear, or, for after your
    desire,
A vibrant blue that billows to your wrists?
It alters what you say, the clothes you wear,

It shouldn't but it does, so keep your shirt on,
It is an aura, and as I cut your cloth
I design caressments gliding through the skin.
Lie cooling in your coffin, tieless like a cricketer,
Tieless like all dead people, or approach your bride
In your groomshirt all belaced and frogged
Frilled, grilled and ribboned like an apple tart,
Devise a lengthy caduceus at your throat
And tuck it down your trousers, or perch
A moony moth to browse your Adam's Apple,
Whatever you do, you need my shirts,
My thought surrounds you from the waist, sign your
    treaties
Without trousers, says the shirtmaker's boy, for all
    I care.

II.
I do not like the vicar's dress.
That blank throat needs a pretty bridge.
His chest is black, his pants cut
Apocryphal, without a bulge. I think the vicar
Is always searching for his missing tie:
It would keep body and soul together.

III.
I will not design my ties for hearty drinkers!
Let the throat have its passage, let the nimble
Apple perform its wedding, and let it be seen
That the dark beer sinks below the head
And as the talk rises from the chest
Buttons and collar are an irrelevance.

IV.
He claims to control storms
By knotting and unknotting suitable ties, I ask him
Might he wish the chest cut bare? Yes, he replies,
But not too bare as he loves the rain to beat
And loves the clinging panels of the shirt
As it grows darker and drenched, as though the skin
Were a child peeking out at the storm from lighted
    windows.

V.
I will sell some women ties if they promise to wear
Soft collars like their satin thighs.
Why shouldn't they practise having a third leg there
To fill the opening up and declare to all
Noli me tangere, sometimes I am a man too.
How much is redeemed also by the affectionate
    parody
Of collar, tie, pinstripe and gangster-tilted trilby.

VI.
They wash the murderer, and soap his head
To shave it, they prepare him like a priest
To connect him to the mains
And flush his bad sad soul along the great wires
That warm and light the houses. Our lamps dim,
He's gone, a glimpse of wings
Flashes across the TV screen, his bright eye
Burns for an instant in that filament.
The scoured corpse sits upright, enthroned,
And completely dressed - except for its tie.
I do not like the grey shirt, but it is open,
No one is sent to the next world with his tie on,
The soul has enough to do to get out of this city
Along the straight cables without going round and
    round
Its daily knot, only that morning
Tied to the naughty face with a shaving-mirror.

VII.
He knots his ample foulard and signs his will.
Strength, beauty, custom and forethought
In a slip-knot, in a hangman's tool.

VIII.
Nobody goes to bed with his tie on either,
Neither he nor she; no pyjama
Threads any cord through its snug flannelette collar.
To die or ejaculate everyone bares his throat,
To let the old life out of the windy passages,
To let the new life in through the wide-open legs.

IX.
Tying his tie, it is the way of the world,
His father taught his fingers to settle the knot
On the soft shirt; untying his tie
It is the way of the next world, his mother loosened it
And got him ready for his bath, taught him
How to undress for the night, using
Undoing, weakly fingers after the long day,
The throat cool, the slight musk of time
Rising from his flesh out of the fresh-turned cleavage,
As he sees how near this garment is now to his
    woman's clothes,
His man's tits glowing like new love in the folds.

The Half-House

A dry brown bush feathered with mosquitoes.
A ruined room with a river running through the end
    of it.
Tablecloths trailing into the fast water.
A silver tureen rolling and clanging among the river
    pebbles.

A billiard table's drenched green meadow
On which the mushrooms have set out an ivory game,
Their scent of salt meat mingles with the nettles';
Ant-scented nettles; the door swings on blackness
Of a white refrigerator like snow among the brambles
That have stopped the clock with yellow fire
On the marble mantlepiece, next to the crucifix
That has budded, its figure missing, like a white
    shadow.

That rustling in the bushes, is it a thrush
Or the small brown Christ sprinting among the pine-
    needles,
In the other half of the house, the little Jesus
Tanned and hard like Robinson Crusoe, shooting
For food rabbits and mice with a string of horsehair
And a gull-feather bow, the hand-wounds
Almost healed in the hard hunter's hands.
He has got into the library, lights
Cooking-fires from the ruined books, tries to pick
Pictures of Mary off the printed pages

(Though, in a fix, he can rip the scabs off
And light a fire with the blood in his veins,
Or scare night-animals by waving his thundering
    hands.)

He smells like a field-Christ.
Like a fertile field the Lord has blessed.

24

Two of the Worlds

I.

From much handling of diapers, I am covered in
    warts.
From much washing of clothes, my tears have
    become suds.
From much sawing of wood, I have macabre dandruff.
From much counting of money, my nails have grown
    silver.
From much watching of TV, my spectacles have
    grown dark.
From much arguing with you, my teeth have grown
    black and my tongue chalky.
From much handling of poisons, I am covered in
    scales.
From much astronomical calculation, I have become
    a star.

II.

And these women, their blouses –
They walk in their flowers and their stripes,
    flourishes, mad fruits
They walk past papered like comics with all our
favourite colours
Like nursery walls reminding you of the room inside
    each one of them

They change these blouses with their garish pages,
    they alter all their stories
Against the flowery paper they glide through the walls
    of houses

In this house she drifts, one of the honeymoon ghosts
    of the house
Or the happy blouse hangs over the back of the chair
    and she is dead or in bed.

The Dreaming Jewels

On my wedding-day that snowed

(My red ring with the white star
Cracked in it) my custom
To scrutinise the snow
To find that patterned crack

Never found it
Until my wedding-day that snowed

Everywhere!

I matched them on the hencoop and the big holly

On my whiskers and the pasture

I reached up into the sky
And plucked the next one down

Again

They matched, heaven matched them

We exchanged rings
My white stone grew a red geometry heart
Her ruby ring melted on the sheets
The engraved mausoleum burst.

And My True Love
Was Blind

(God, solus)

My friend, sleeping in the apples.

Half the treasure was invisible, half the treasure

Impossible. He is strolling
In the garb that suits him

Blue hood, crisp beard.

I see his perfume in the shadow.
An abyss of wisdom and a cloud of unknowing.

To watch my vows return!
It is a siesta, an interval.
He strolls on inwardly.

I watch from the sky, I watch from the dew-pond.

Nothing hurts.

Invisible, the half of my treasure.

The Graveyard Diploma

In the garden
There is the Hebrew fountain
Fat yod he vau he
Letters of water
Literate plashing

My bed is made up
In the unswept ossuary

A gallery of framed death-warrants

A sepulchral university

A ripple down my penis from the grave-snakes

From the moon inside her blouse
Tin-light pours from her cloudy buttonholes

There is a silver moon-blush
A cloud passes over her face, and clears

I strike my encampment
And move out of the mound-marsh
The mists wave goodbye to me
Grey fish

They are dew suddenly:
I strike out over the wide water that supports me

The conscious fresco quivers
He springs over the threshold
And lands, teeth chattering.

Love is Neither Word, Deed Nor Blouse

My hand in her blouse-breast lost its power,
Its breast had my hand's power.
The poetry they wear, the clothes they write!
Her blouse pretties itself with a zig-zag tie,
Something cancelled, not quite cancelled

Married in that blouse!
                              that self-environment
Something between a river and a room
Its surface crammed with currents

Something between a habitation and a sail!
That voyaging blouse
The sleeves mean marriage
It clings to the mirror like a silver moth

Light pours from buttonholes and cuffs

What life alights in that vivacious house!

To the Known God

Priests! you should not have left conjuring.
It is a healthy, relaxing art.
It is good to move among swarms of magic.

It is good to follow service day by day
And woo the god of that church with ceremonial
    suppers
With hymns ringing in the stone and blessed water
And see nothing and feel nothing
And pray to the unknown god

But it is also good for one learned in vestments
To visit the bonfire crackling like a released
    footprint
In the green wood and the quiet persons gathering,
Polished antlers, glowing in the firelight,
Who speak to their priests as equals, some of whom
    are gods
With straight spines and animal heads

It is good to have one god running the daylight
And another running through the dark on great thews
    of venison
Who dines on the cooked venison
Who runs with the does made of venison
Who speaks with a venison tongue
Who created venison for his pleasure and yours.

Cicada Singing

The child often sings in its sleep
He must sing without interruption
He sees the ladydoctor's clear conscience
This is the font of lucidity, its smell
The dead people picked to pieces in the rainfall
Swallowed by the trees
Tuned by the cicadas
Standing on each leaf
Dead Indians
Dead Americans
Frontiersmen
Fighters for the revolution
A dead student or two
Still singing
The child sleeps and sings under the trees
The trees sing a song with veins in it
A song with fruits and marbles and clear conscience
   in it
A song like a tuning-in to silence
It rises to a pitch and falls silent
The trees stand companionable
The child asleep like a tree, singing

You walk into the wood, it tunes itself to you,
You pick up the child still sleeping, you sing to it

Sabbat

come dancing
the men in black and white like governesses
the ladies clothed in sparking shrouds
unclothed at last'.

so much money'. no more need to work, or dress.

Mother has died and become the Food Hall at
    Harrods
with its French-cut veal, German Bratwurst,
langoustes and langoustines –

no washing up'. no thousand sequins to polish
no shirts to boil
they live it up at last, foxtrot up and away

to their own music'.

among the asses pastured in quiet among the hollies
the green-steel leaves and the hide-grey meadows
silvered asses pastured in the moonlight

the synodic Bald Mountain lighted up
all the furrows and watercourses clean and brilliant

I hear the smoke bumping against the sides of the
    chimney
the freed witches bounding upwards, the palais empty.

The Navy's Here

Power sliding off great faces of water,
Power in flat sheets rising,
Ornamental waters giving up their power,
The Jewish Fountain, of fat and thin letters,
The plain English water-plots.

A woman traces the plan of a battleship.

After our small hooves clattering all night
Our pinsize toothmarks in the butter,
Waking with tiny cogwheels in the eye-corners
A woman traces the plan of a battleship.

The dockyard swings the last plate in,
The earth bleeds green upwards.

We sail the seas invisible in our battleships.
The sun dazzles our gun-barrels.
Our navy's cogwheels are tabernacles.
Our shiny hooves sail ten thousand.
We trample the green seas, snorting.

It was the tininess of the hooves stampeded her.
Now we are church-sized mice, nickel-plated.
Ten thousand of us make up one mouse.

The woman stands at the quayside, gently laughing.
When we ask for it, there is a door in the water
And a wavering staircase. She stands at the foot.
Since we were sailors we become salt. We are sea-
   sized.
You can taste us everywhere. We sting the eyes.

Serious Readers

All the flies are reading microscopic books;
They hold themselves quite tense and silent
With shoulders hunched, legs splayed out
On the white formica table-top, reading.
With my book I slide into the diner-booth;
They rise and circle and settle again, reading
With hunched corselets. They do not attempt to taste
Before me my fat hamburger-plate, but wait,
Like courteous readers until I put it to one side,
Then taste briefly and resume their tomes
Like reading-stands with horny specs. I
Read as I eat, one fly
Alights on my book, the size of print;
I let it be. Read and let read.

From the Answers to Job

The ghost that rapes, photographed suddenly on the
    stairs.
I see him climbing the stairs in flashes
I see him enter the bedroom in white flashes
In flashes he is unbuckling his workman's belt
He stands behind me in flashes as I write
I have risen from my bath and towelled myself dry
I am wrapped about in my clean towelling dressing-
    gown
I write about the ghost and he enters me in flashes
He sits in my clean body as on a human throne
I am the ghost who rapes who comes back for more
Who cannot rest because he cannot quite do it
I am the man who rapes, I have a ghost that needs to
    die
I seek the woman who will kill my ghost, she needs to
    be broken

The rain begins and each drop is charged with
    knowledge
There is the ghost who smiles in the river
And the ghost who eats dung because he is a mushroom
The ghost who eats corpses because she is grass
The ghosts which eat grass because they are beefs
The ghosts who are beefeaters because they are men
The ghosts who eat coal because they are flames
The ghost who rapes steps into my body
Newly-clean out of the quick flame of the candle into
    my body

38

He sits as on a throne in the slow flame of my body
The slow waxy flame of my body
The candle looks over my shoulder, my right
 shoulder, my left shoulder,
The candle creaks and spits and it says 'grease'
No it says 'ease' no it says 'jeeze' and very quietly
 'us'
It eases us, peering over my shoulder
In the mirror, like the slant eye of a beast.
The shadows in the draught swirl about my head,
They are trying to wrench my face backwards
Into a ram's face with great horns of shadow,
A wise goat-face with a great muzzle, with moist
 nostrils,
With a little string of phlegm whipping in the left
 nostril
A ram's face with pupils of black stone and pleated
 gold foil
I raise the candle placing it between the goat's horns
Which are moons its flame like an eye open between
 moons
I ease you the lips of leather whisper I ease you
A little string of blood whipping in the left nostril.

The Barbers

I.
With just a rubbing of sun
The flies come doddering out
Upon the windowpanes and mirrors like old men
Tottering through the landscapes
With several walking-sticks
Their long hair dirty with winter
On their way to the barber's.

II.
The barber cuts the beard
It is a mode of fathering.
We control our face-hair in Oneida county.
Never have your beard cut by a younger man.
A room of thrones and transformations.
The flies totter out pale-faced, clean-shaven,
A man sheds years in front of this gilded mirror
You can stuff a pillow with his soft years.
It is also where the fedora gangsters
Start out from the sunny sidewalk
Pumping charred holes into the shrouded shoulders.

III.
The Chinese have five officials of the human body:
The mouth, nose, ear, eye and eyebrow,
Communicating with each other by means of hair,
Formed or unformed messengers of hair.

The strong eye-brow is the preserver of life,
The black balance-needle, and when
We wish to depict a man we do so with hair!
His loins or constitution. Jesus
Was a barber not a carpenter; his brother
The trapper creates small cold corpses
That have outworn their need for the hair
He sells in head-caps, mufflers and potent top-coats.

IV.
The one clean-shaven like a white grape
Affronts no man: he is an egg. The barber
Bishops this rendering monkish, Lord
Of the Numerous Transformations of Skins
And Renewal Coming of Itself.
We cut and trim to make our plots
And express ourselves in repose.
Where is that man with the ankle-length beard?
He has stepped out of it. Is he
That youth with the 'tash?
Or that monk in the suit?

V.

The nibbling digits, the glittering scissor-blades
Busy like feeding fish among the scalps,
The whetted razor on the supple strops,
The pungent flasks of vivid toiletries,
The flat condoms in casual packets sold
To any comer with face-hair.

VI.

He renews his face each morning, shaving
Round his moustache, male destiny;
We do not tattoo the face to make our blazon,
It is a choice and selection of hair.
I try out beards in the bearded mirror,
Watchful as Zapata, pure as Solzhenitzyn,
His stiff upper lip shaved very naked,
Dapper as Van Dyke, pointless as Empson,
And in my own person
Laugh as an egg laughs.
I want to laugh
With teeth among the hair.

VII.

Three-day stubble, an abrasive sight,
He is my Dad, and the skin is sharklike;
Roughness is a quality of the mountain and the shark.

VIII.
He grows his beard like hibernation
In the springtime shaves it off,
The spring forces spruce his face,
He is a calendar, and this barometer
Bristles like the sun's rays or streams limp like
    rain
As the seaweed on the hatstand assists the tourist.
His eyes float like planets above this bearded sea
Innocent, remote from weather or puberty.

IX.
Here is his coffin. And here the barber comes
With his other coffin full of all the hair
He shed since his father took him for a shave.
That was like a first communion.
This is needed for the resurrection.

X.
Do you know Jesus? Does he wear a beard?
Is his skin soft, with a little silky cobweb?
Has his voice broken yet, does he gangle?
Is he the Adolescent with whey skin and brown voice?
Has the Egg dropped, and are the emissions
    nocturnal?
Do you say Horus Horsecollar, eternal God,
Coltish teenager with the too-large collars
Because his Mother the Widow still buys his shirts
Remembering by this the size of her husband's bull
    neck?

XI.
Over the snowy meadow in the gazing sky
The hairy stars palpitate assembled
For their winter work, computing spring.
Orion steps up out into the air
With his fleshy sword, and buckler of the three kings.
When he lies down in the long coarse grass
He is the sexual giant of the English hill, * but here
Is that a goatee tickling at his ancient chin,
The lean Orion in the Yankee sky?

*The Cerne Abbas Giant.

44

Snowmanshit

or
Our Six-Armed Ice-Device
(Winter in Upstate New York: Hamilton)

I.
The black cloudy sculptor in the sky
Carves innumerable six-armed works
They fall gently to the ground, all different.

He intends comment on whiteness.

Sunset dyes these works all reds
All browns, all purples,
All icy blues,
Anything but white;
He says he will see through them, too,
Eventually, rotund
Critic of snowflakes.

II.
Since the shavings of this masterpiece are so great
What a masterpiece there must be up in the sky!

Or perhaps the masterpiece is already here on earth
And the six-armed shavings are the great work
And what is above in the black clouds not much good

Or maybe the masterpiece in the sky is too great
And too black for our eyes
Content
With small magnificent
Six-sided etchings,

Frost prints

And six-spiked signatures.

III.
The black sculptor lifts a massive piece of silver
Dripping and shining out of the sea

And carves it; his shavings sleet.

Down here, my watch sings in chirps like a bird
Spitless song.

In the sky he is carving an immense white watch
It has no hands, the minutes fall whitely from it,
Immense six-second minutes falling in steady pulses.

IV.
In her bright blouses, her cuffs
Bright as lamps she carries to her face, her food;
In her dark blouses, the blinding pearl of cuff-
    buttons;
Outside the house, the endless rain
Of six-sided buttons creates
One bright earth-blouse complete.

V.
The sun focusses to a point in the icicle it is
    destroying,
In the tree of icicles each one contains a point of the
    sun:
Bright smut destroying harvests of icicles.
Now the night sleeves each bough in black ice;
Down the long dark tunnels the day approaches.

VI.
The sun-links rattling silently on the lake's wavelets;
The moon seizes the lake like an integral white
    instrument;
The moon fills the earth with white mirrors, this
    water
Has observed gorgons all night long.

VII.
The palm of the hand is no liar;
Only
A dead hand clutches ice until morning;
Falling on the warm mudra the spiky snow
Disarms

All the house-roofs clench icicles until morning
Like armies of my friends frozen under water;
How powerful your friends are,
Snowflake, born to die on a warm Zennist palm.

VIII.
On a sunny snowy afternoon near to sunset,
The woods purple as wrack,
The snowflakes begin again, like small white
Fortresses toppling slowly, like
Small white grenadiers cartwheeling stiffly
Out of the shattered plans of some frozen campaign.

IX.
Stripped water-piano of ice-strings and thin black
    keys;
Cinema-organ of rainbow icicles rising as the
    headlights move in;
Each glass-branch has a skinny black vein in it;

Glistener, I snap a corpse-candle from you in the
    moonlight,
Moontree of water-telescopes.

X.
The snowflakes
Whirling their six arms
Like windmills of mirror
Revolve snowy streams and ice-pines without end,
Alight, adjust them. I walk out to the snowman
Who is seen six ways by every settling mirror;
White babel of imagery, my warm
Black coat would simplify you.

XI.
The white snowdunes
Have blue undershadows
As white women
Have blue dresses
Which blow along
Blue shadowy couches
And blue beds where
All night white
Glows invisibly.

XII.
The snow
Hooks up
Crusty animal masks

The shaggy trees
Swagged with faces
Snow-fox
Arctic bear

Shock-haired trophies
With mournful evergreen eyes.

XIII.
The snowlight of the meadows:
Like a camera suddenly opened,
The film stark-naked;
Or the death-mouth breaks open;
Bleached photos of my lungs
Still cling to the pathways.

XIV.
More big flakes like gentle dabbing gloves
Which are six-fingered, wet;
Which are like old people, nothing left
But white hair, white whisker;

They come in their millions, in their phalanxes,
Like blanched ants from crushed black nests,

Like dazzling spiders astride six-stranded
  gossamers,
Like mass-produced blouses blowing about in the
  shattered windows
After the end of the world, all the
Empty shirts and blouses
Marching out of the shops and crying white peace !

XV.
Before it docked we watched winter work in the lake
Like a warped yacht ice came sailing,
Bleached planks in the depths nailing themselves
  together,
White sails sewing underwater.

The whole earth is now sheeted and sailed with snow,
All America like a full-rigged ship with sails full
Of the harsh cold breath of old people
Coughing with a six-sided cough all winter

All Hallows celebrated in a white cathedral
Without shadows and decorated with white banners
White pews upholstered softly with white hassocks
A fair of white tombs and quiet white carousels
And white guns to shoot for white prizes
And black midnights in which to sail our yacht of
  snow
On whose livid decks we leave many footprints which
  are too small.

XVI.
Snowflakes on a sunny noon, sailing down
So fast on to the black lake
Like white letters on a black page
That melt as I read.
I am reading, I know it,
But I have forgotten all but this page
And then
More fall on the white plain like white letters
Adding more knowledge to the fatness of a fat white
    book
Too full to be opened, too brilliant to be read.

XVII.
He knows the hills
The snowflakes pass into him
As they pass into the tree-branches
Lining his bones in full view of everybody
Lining his dream-body
Whitening his skull publicly and shattering it
Into six-armed bits, the slopes of the flying
    snowmountains
Glittering with shattered comrades.

XIX.
The child in its bright blue nylon-fleece snowcoat
Crams with woollen mittens much snow

Between dingied teeth neat as frost, through rose-
  lips,
Then triumphant in cold air looses smoking six-sided
  piss.

XX.
I carve a snowoman with a table-knife; from a tin cup
I baptise her with long ice-hair,
My hand shakes and she grows a tinkling beard,
I have two warm blue marbles for her icy glare;
I wedge my sweaty black hat on her head,
Winter glues it there.
What a fuss this whitebeard has not made,
Not a syllable, they are a personage,
They are the Old One because they were first of all
Among the glaciers, among the cold centuries,
I wish they would have their warm red period.

XXI.
The mirror-lake no longer
Lets the white clouds slip away, the lake
Is frozen cloud

The frosts turn firs into pinnacles, high-pitched ice.

Now, the morning - warm and dry:
How hard it rains inside the steep green trees!

XXII.
More snow comes pacing down
More pieces for the cathedral, more components
Annexed to the icechurch: chapels, cloisters,
Mistchapterhouses, enormous
Water-set for constructing snowarchitecture, and
    now, surely not

When the house of water stands so tall, when the
    cloudmountains
Are so nearly reconstructed on our fields, should
    there be still more
Great flakes pacing like white monks,
Crystalline six-sided chants,
Symmetrical mandala-prayers of white solicitude
Fitting perfectly each to each
Petition to petition

Asking that the house of water may still build depths
That lakes may one day set rooms of sky deep down
And resourceful rivers mine green lands again.

XXIII.
The snow comes pacing, like a priest
Who is nothing but white robes, whose hours
Fit together like a great loose watch
Of cogs obeyed by everyone. How many die of him
Snowing on the white hairs even of Red Men
Who grow white-skinned in their age
And travel underground, in many forms.

Insects had their Choice and Became Insects

The prison hums like purgatory with the bees in it
The bees in the prison stone, the mountain of bees,
The prisoners have transformed into bees in the
    sandy stone.

They make honey from the flowers in the courtyard
The flowers have broken up the stone flags
The stone laundry-trough is sudsing with flowers
The bees make thick sweet honey from them

That boulder has soaked up the cicada-hum
Millions of years, it vibrates for ever;
Beetles like stouted winebottles that climb boulders.

The thistledown is a wisp, nothing
But a crimson prick and a silky white beard,
The grasshopper sits like a shadow in the depths
Eternally winding his watch in the iridescent depths

That is a necroscope, that ivy of berries;
That bird-turd spreads fringed locust-wings;
The prisoners shout! one of their number

Has made it over the wall on fringed wings.
The warder stops winding his watch all of thirty
    seconds.

The Doctrine of the Window

There are windows, little sliding traps
Of white wood people push exhausted money through
Summoned by bill. There are clear squares
Summating landscapes with the help of chattering
   highballs;
There are dark high windows, behind which
Great novels are written by young persons
Lacking the price of candles; there are low-down
   bays
For grim-jawed women in buns of sandy hair
Whose knitting has overgrown them like trellises;
There are waterfalls, whose ever-roar
Reminds visiting hermits of distant hermitages,
Through whose speeding glass the black mountain
   looks back at you;

And there is this doctor in spectacles
Sitting behind his desk like his own high windows,
No he is a clear door, you saw your reflection first
Then you climbed out of him twenty-seven floors up
   into weather
Of city streets that darken as gazes dive,
Office windows flashing with eyes that plunge;
The cops arrive in cars screaming like suicides.

But if you prefer to remain in-windows, this
Glass of water is Eve with her straight face
And clear depths; if Adam saw water
Standing up on its own like this, not flowing
And not falling, neither living nor dead water
He'd run a mile to his psychiatrist out of the Garden
Frantically knocking at his french-window
Where like a reflection the doctor prepares him for
    the fall.

Insect Statues

The dead cicadas
Staring at nothing
With nothing
Through their horny glasses
Perched in crannies
Bark niches
Completely shed-empty
Drunk up by their comrades
Whose armour sang
As they drank
And who sit singing
Drilling the leaves
Scraping their musical bellies
With sugar crystallising on their jaws
The tree singing infested
Bleeding sweet juices
Song-fuel

Its green seeds
Fly on the wind
That brings the song
These plump seeds fly
On leathern wings
This maple
Has a voice made of sugar.

A Twelvemonth

In the month called Bride
there is pale spectral honey
and in-laws made of chain-mail and whiskers.

In the month called Hue-and-Cry
green blood falls with a patter
and the pilchard-shoal flinches.

The month called Houseboat
is for conversing by perfume
and raising beer-steins;
great stone-and-foam masks.

In the month called Treasurechest
snails open jalousies onto their vitals:
pinecones, pollen-packed.

In the month called Brickbat
the sea is gorgeous with carpets
of orange jelly-fish squads;
and the people ride.

The month called Meatforest
is for flowers in the abattoirs,
catafalques for the steers.

In the month known as William
we watch the deer grazing on seaweed;
police open the strongroom of Christ.

In the month called Clocks
the poets decide
whether they shall draw salary,

And in the month called Horsewhip
they pluck their secret insurance
from the rotting rafters.

In the Mollycoddle month
barbers put up bearded mirrors
and no-one is allowed to die.

In the month called Yellow Maze
all the teddy-bears
celebrate their thousandth birthday.

In the month called Sleep-with-your-wife
the sea makes a living
along this quiet shore, somehow.

Plain Poems of Change in February

I.

Caesar died
The boy pared his nails
Rome fell
The boy crossed his legs
Pope Paul crumbled
Boy, we know you,
Give us parole.

II.

On Easter Day
I walked in the park
A window sun-flashed
I thought of a distant flat
And a woman writing.

III.

The long bones on the path
By the strenuous stream
Woke me with a start.
I had been travelling the winter
Merely pacing
Now I begin to run
She cannot be far away.

IV.
Why at my age
Did I perch in that crotch?
Did that tree teach me to sing?
Did it teach me to slither?
Suddenly I had an audience
Three ladies mooning and a black policeman

V.
There are inky fingermarks
In 'The London Shakespeare'
There is a trail of them
Through 'Exploring Poetry' and 'The Act of Creation'
There is a geological hammer
With an inky handle
And the typescript of a novel
In the green chair
The wedding-ring is in bed already
Snoring, the right road home
Printed across the books.

VI.
The cat rubs his tom-bottom
On the mould under the thin leaves,
Last year's rose-leaves,
He prepares for Spring.
The first condition of the ghost
Is that it returns.

VII.
Deep in the found night
At the window of dreams
The thriving greenhouse
Of the lost day's orchids.

VIII.
There are eight fruits
The quince is in the ballroom and part of the
    sandwiches
The banana is walking through the front door its skin
    limp on the threshold
The apple is in the bathroom, they are bobbing with it
    in the basin
The cherries are in the bedroom and are part of a
    game of spitting and adornment
The plum has caused a misfortune since the stone has
    been swallowed
The mistletoe is in a conspicuous place, wall flowers
    watch it like hawks
The pear is only a painted pear but it is worth six
    thousand pounds
The grapes are wet and are lying forgotten in the
    colander
I am watching them for their profound wet duskiness
    in the kitchen
But my ears stretch in spirals through the ballroom,
    bedrooms etc.

IX.
I like that wet lady in the muslin
Who catches fishes that can breathe water
And men who cannot.

Notes and Squeals

Checkov, at Spok's station, moved no buttons,
The mad eyes dripping tears, the fly,
Where no fly should be, snatched at his sleeve,
And on the screens of guidance in the immaculate
    panels
Some effeminate leper smashed a wasp, there
    formed
An advertisement for winter beer. On the planet
    outside
Their sealed-in mikes heeded a tolling bell;
It bonged from the bulbous mountain that ran with
    lava
And a man bright as berries stepped smartly forward
With an unsigned peace-treaty. Under a rotund star
The Enterprise, shaped like its creator's brain
Hanging five foot six above the vinous earth
Spoke inwardly: 'Spok! where did that fly come from?
It uses oxygen. In the Federation's name
I order you to swat it, peaceably. Then land.'

Hard-Beaked Toymakers

The hard beaks of the toymakers want blood.
They are all drinking the blood of babies.
The babies with cheeks red as radishes
Wish nothing harm, except toys that drink blood.

A sudden wind flaps the leaves
Of the frost trees on the glass.

The baby's hand flat on the glass
Melts a water-print, the baby's fingers
Fell a water-forest, with water-monkeys.

The baby looks long and deep into his handprints.
The world is a jewel, hanging in black flesh,
The street light glows orange, pumps like a heart,
The world is made of windows, with babies
Watching sternly from hand-prints.

Everything you have is made with hands.
The table pounds you with hammers
The pack of cards scratches you with pens
The book sews your lips shut
The toy rooster for cash
Sucks your blood with a little tooth of bright tin.

Trashabet

'*Wabi* is the spirit of poverty... appreciation of
what most consider to be the commonplace...
something hitherto ignored being seen for the
precious thing it is...'.
Lucien Stryk: *Zen Poems of China and Japan.*

A is for ash, which is primary trash. With it I can
make bash, cash, dash, fash, gash, hash, lash,
mash, pash, rash, sash but not wash.

B is for buttons, which are a cross between numbers
and persons. Snip a button from Joey's shirt, and it
is Joey. Snip six buttons, and you have spots to
arrange in an equilibrated pattern of Joey. I possess
buttons stolen from everybody I have ever known;
they are as good as photographs. I have filled four
large grocery boxes with the buttons, and I recognise
each one personally.

C is for cat's fur. If I rub this old plastic
haberdasher's hand with cat's fur, it will pick up
light buttons by electricity.

D is for dead wood. Sawdust, and lathe-shavings. I
have my great beetle stroll over the yellow sawdust
in a black dish. He leaves marks that I can interpret,
I read them off as stories or drawings. Lathe-
shavings may be dyed, and made into wigs.

E is for egg-shells. Glueing dust-bin eggshells
together is good sport for a poor man, but there is
always one piece left over.

F is for dead flies. I have one wall in my shack
studded like tacks with flies' heads dried and glued
to the matchboard, as other men have halls of
trophies.

G is for grit. It flies everywhere in the summer,
when the wind blows off the dunes. I think sometimes
of my house and its treasures riding a tidal sea of
shifting grit.

H is for happenings. When I recognise a button, when
I complete an egg-shell, when I sell a wood-shaving
dog dyed black-and-white, when I triumph over a
muscular bluebottle with a rolled-up paper marked
'clubhouse', these are happenings.

I is for myself. I am Midas, but not greedy. There
is nothing which does not interest me, providing it
costs no money.

J is for jamjars. I use these as a sorcerer uses his
glassware. A dead mouse in a carefully-sewn shroud
rests on seven layers of grit; the particles are
graded by size and colour. The shroud is the silk

lining of part of my overcoat, it has a hood. The claws are crossed on the tiny chest, the jar is sealed with a page of the bible tied with waxed string. With this machine, that brims with invisible stench like evil prayers; with this corpse, that threads with silvery maggots like new guesses, that, when the maggots have pupated and risen again, buzzes with tiny voices like a church of the resurrected; with this life-machine I curse rich monks and church commissioners.

K is for Kraft paper that prolongs the life of shoes, that screens the shadow-theatre of my windows. When I wish fresh air, I punch a hole with my fist.

L is for Livingstone Waterstone, which is paraffin wax. When I have a candle, the shadows flow through my boxes and rags and the air feels good like crackling water, and my house is a river of rags of light. On other occasions I never see the night, since I wake at dawn and bed at sunset. Livingstone also crackles and whispers to me. From his scratches in the air, I read off pictures and tales as well.

M is for mousetrap, that provides me with corpses. Another wall is crammed with the bright-eyed, sharp-nosed trophy heads. I used coal-chips for the eyes.

N is for the near-miss I had when I caught cold from fishing in the quarry. I lay on fire, like a horizontal Livingstone burning flames of sweat. Then all my poverty was living vivacity, without any effort of invention at all on my part, and I burned in a world that had never heard of money. This was a near-miss. I near-missed being a holy fool, I near-missed losing all my pride. There was nothing to fight.

O is for objects of no significance and great interest that have survived millions of years. In the quarry I find the fossil of a wave-ripple, the fossil of the common five-winged button-urchin, the petrified crater of a rain-drop in mud.

P is for urine, and for my staff of life, my living waterstone, that, gripped in my hands and radiating its sunny beams, reflects: I am a fruit, I am a stem; as its nitrogen sinks into the soil.

Q is for queer, which I was, and hetero, which I was, and solitary, which I am, and I preserve the best features of both. I live with myself, who am a member of my own sex; and I live with the moneyless ghost, who is a ragged girl, and who enters into more beings than a human woman can. She is the buttons and the urine, and the drenched shirt, and the livingstone and the near-miss.

R is for arse, which she enters when she is in my fingers, and which she leaves as stable-gas. If you do not understand this, I cannot explain it any further to you.

S is for shit, which no, I do not make trophies of, nor are they my babies. I dry it for fires and I spread it for manures, and I shall use it for hair-tonic or salad dressing if I please without asking permission.

T is for the architecture of my bed-sitting space. There is a pillar, which supports a roof. The pillar is of wood, and the roof is of iron, which is corrugated for strength and to shed the rain. The cross-piece runs north and south, the pillar penetrates the earth, which is the past and the future, and rises into the present. During my near-miss it was wreathed with vines and nests of grapes in which golden birds chattered.

U is for my uvula when I sing and my upraised arms when I dance around my tent-pole, my mouth full of white buttons.

V is for the forked twig in which I light my livingstone.

71

W is for the three weathers of the moon, I grow with
her, I stand still in her light, my thought decays,
and in the decay flash new silvery guesses; and for
*W*riting this alphabet, which is taking me to *X* the
cross-roads I am approaching for *Y* should I remain
poor when *Z* the silvery flash-guess strikes the
world to how a child is all-interested and his body
made of breathing jewels, but this

> Takes me round the circle to *A*
> Which is for ambition and ashes.

An Alphaladybet

She lifted out the silver bell and struck it with the hammer. It rang, Beware, *A*melia, beware. *Love was many red curtains drawing aside in the horse-scent of a greenhouse.*

*B*ianca fell into the well. She shrieked and then she sang to keep warm. The well still sings. I peered over the parapet; she swam the rippling disc. *Love was a water-snake, turning through billows.*

*C*harity will not speak during group therapy. She dances. This week she dildo–danced with the haft of her umbrella in front of us all. The grossness of her behaviour enforced charity on her fellow patients. *But my charity was a lie on the silk that split deep within us as we loved.*

The Lady of the *D*inosaurs dreams me. She casts bulky vegetarian shadows. The white fleas of these shadows march into her battles like horny transparent parrots, to their clatter of knives and forks. They return from her battles engorged like red–cheeked sentries with purple coats. Then her shadows are curse-coloured. She dismisses all her other animals and turns to me. She opens her mouth in a sudden command. *Love was being boiled until all the skins were soft.*

*E*stelle carves, in a very hard green stone, snails
that have the graceful heads of swans. Her sleeves
are white and full and she wears crimson gloves to
protect her flesh from the trim-saws and gouges.
Love was the admixture of dune-sands.

*F*elicity married a butcher who died of a heart-attack
in the abattoir. They laid him on the bed; there was
fresh blood on his hands and in his hair. The pietà of
a butcher is the death of death. He comes to her in
dreams clothed in silver and dripping silver from his
eyelids. He touches her anaemic breast with a black
knife; she is surrounded suddenly with a pleasurable
stench of human milt, which lingers as she wakes.
It lingers; love was like the breaking and running of eggs.

Somebody buried *G*ilda in the chicken-run. She
transferred into the eggs via the worms. The yolk of
my egg sprang from its shell and stood poised on my
spoon – a naked golden woman. Then before I could
shut my mouth she dived down my throat. *Love was
shitting a complete daffodil in blossom-lust - rootlets, bulb,
leaf-blades, tremulous scent and glad yellow.*

Learned *H*umility dons her snail helmet, and crawls
down the street. She is always ready to leave. She
urinates like a man, standing up. Just as

unexpectedly, she makes love like an angel (my body fills with the beating of wings). Her contradictions humble me. *Love with her is being caressed by a tall cool flower that is dark.*

*I*ris, which means 'rainbow', is the track this messenger leaves on the air as she flies to the gods, though she is blind, and used to making lace without using her eyes. *Love with her is sighted, the singing head contemplates the brown river as it moves rapidly upstream to the source, which is very cool and small.*

*J*essica said to us: 'Magic brings peace and mirth. If it does not, it is not magic, and not worth having.' She waved her hand. The rain stopped. But the rainbow still spanned the garden. The vicar, perplexed, scratched his head. Then we all laughed together. *Love with her is wavelets catching up with great waves and turning their crests over, and on the white crests there is writing.*

*K*irsty is losing her beautiful raven hair. She resolves that she will weave it into an evening dress, and refuse to wear a wig. Her bald pate will shine in the subdued light of expensive restaurants. *Love is watching the world in a cool mirror that beats.*

The Honourable Mrs *L*enice *L*ytton-Scythe seduced me. She raised her arm in its thick tweed and pointed to a small black leather diary on a top shelf. 'Will you...?' she asked. As I reached up, she reached down. This woman with the square-toed shoes imparted a mother-naked shock; I cannot explain this. Dawn frosted the windows. 'We must leave for the hospital now,' she said, destroying a white forest with a suede finger. *Love with her paced like a clock-face written by hand.*

Night after night Sister *M*oira would sit bolt upright in bed shouting 'Antlers! The Street of Antlers! The Blood!' During the day however, her very suitable behaviour earned her the nickname of 'Sister Emollient'. *Love was rain-claws over the skin, and no orgasm.*

*N*esta waves the green flag and the train moves out. There is a flurry of rain from the north. She sighs, and pulls her cap-peak lower, hurries to the ticket-office, where she is discussing the test-match draw with the booking-clerk. If she did not wave her flag, the trains could not move; if the trains did not move, she could neither walk, stand, wave her flag nor breathe. *After that sex, there is a beam of sunlight that travels with my eyes and comes to rest on certain objects*

in her room: a cheap vase, a newspaper, the engagement
ring that spins unmoving on her hand.

Oona says, 'The spark in the dolphin's heart is the
spark at the heart of each fragment of the mountain
of flint.' The trumpeters riff and the people listen as
Oona's fish become the world's harvest of good meat
to the blessed: 'The mackerel leap into our hands
and the good fish-blood runs down our throats.' She
wears a hat which is made to look like a calm face
with a pointed beard. *Her love is not bestowed; to*
break the egg would destroy her.

Under a grainy gunpowder-cloak, Peace wears
flame-coloured clothes. She knows how to swear
horribly in public around the vulture's crusty anus
and the necrophile kitten. She is the orator the
authorities catch and emprison, it calms them.
She has many siblings, each of whom makes a standing
wave in her cunt for a prison lover to enjoy. Then, at a
peak, this is like the manes of horses running.

Queenie says to me in bed, 'Am I manipulating?'
'No,' I reply, 'you are dreaming.' Or I say to
Queenie in bed, 'I must be dreaming!.' 'No,' she
says, 'you are manipulating.' *This is love.*

Ruth is a small, savage, Zen-minded painter. Zen, or painting, or savagery, or all three must be good for a person, *since her skin dissolves into moths, which flutter unbearably.*

Shirley's first and only orgasm came shortly after she had decided silently to leave her husband. She was incensed by this consummation; flouncing downstairs, she fell and damaged her spine. *Love makes her a baby again, and she cannot walk.*

Tourmaline, the gentle Tourmaline, gathers the cooling ashes. *Never loved.*

Ursula, little bear. *Indeed It danced, and swiped with Its claws, and gobbled the Pudding.*

Veronica watched the white-haired ghost firing the black iron cannon at midnight on the castle ramparts. The rumble and flash were for her alone. Her father, the tomb-throated guide, slept on in the lodge. *Poor Veronica, dreaming of her father primed and fired that cannon.*

Wendy Wet-Dress after her parties lay in the surf, or in the fountain, or stood under the shower, it was invariable. As the crinoline by reverse emphasis drew attention to the cunt within, so her dresses drenched, hollowed and clung. I saw the incident in the draughty surf, she lay as if drowned, the waves washing into her hair, her dress semi-transparent, her breasts looming like the moon. *Only an oaf would have spoiled the picture by entering the water with her, but she attracted those she despised.*

*X*ena. Walking towards the river, we passed the vestry. The door had been left half-open. Empty surplices were hanging inside like large flimsy white flies. 'I wish I were a parson,' said *X*ena, ' and had liturgical dresses to follow the year round.' *She tasted of wine and self-treading grapes.*

*Y*vonne. 'What a young name!.' I thought as I approached the little brown crone lying on her side, whose face was alight from years of sunshine. *Lifting her into bed, she is light as a leather bucket, that grows very heavy as it fills from within.*

Zoe. Without her, everything returns lie for lie. We, her lovers, speak of her as we speak of life. If it is permitted to name the mystery, *she clothes our skins with exterior cunt.* If you understand this, I am as happy for you as I am for myself, but if you do not, then I will ask Zoe to explain it to you further.

An Ape-Button-Cross

A is for an old buttonless flower-ape devouring oak-forests in acorn-form, and for the lilac ashes of the protomartyr. These smell of cat-shit and are mixed with the metal buttons of his collarless robe.

B is for the tense and silent bell-shadow like a button that can sing. It is hanging on its last thread.

C is for the long candles lit nightly for the visiting snakes. Each snake takes up its position wound round a cool shaft, and sips at the flame until sunrise. *C* is for the boulder-crone who is wreathed with yellow peaches and red holly berries that are like buttons made of soft gold and blood.

D is for the imperious dog that ate all of him, but spat out his buttons.

E is for God slipping on his overall of Eyes, buttoning it up, and knowing everything.

F is for flies, the small black hearses that are sometimes spinning sequins and sometimes lazy overcoat buttons undone in the heat. Each grim-jawed equipage gnaws pieces of summer.

G is for ghosts. I have watched the dead faces flower a lifetime of expressions in a night, backwards. As for the Gnats, with only Ghosts and the midnight trees to bite, they have turned to wood, a gust of dolls' eyelashes. Ghosts and gnats are buttonless, and this is why I have passed through the bloodletters at twilight with my face buttoned, I have placed large heavy buttons on the dead eyes to keep them from opening, and I have ensured that the toggles, hasps and screw-down buttons on the coffin-fronts are secure.

H is for the button-nosed head of Socrates, the stone head that sweats and converses, the stone penis that ejaculates glittering quartz-sand, the fluted stone belly-button: you insert your little finger and wish for sand-storms and button-storms.

I is for how often I have noticed that the creator of the universe is represented as a corpse whose shroud is fastened with neither buttons nor ties, in order to allow the free egress and ingress of his great soul.

J is for Jacob's antagonist: the wind! those wings! and the burning judo hold, seized by nostrils and anus, and the rolling limp! The Semite god is no respecter of trouserbuttons.

K is for knockers. Each bristol is knotted to the universe by means of a fine twirling red button.

L is for the place where the lion-cub paces through the black ice, between the glaciers. He claws the arctic mirror for petrifacts of flesh, he observes in it how erotic stars button the sky with far-away bulls, rams, goats, his own kind, and cancer.

M is for Marksmanship, Manger and Mangling. For the young officers, shooting practice this morning with the golden-haired corpse of a farm-girl full of black button-holes; for black Jesus, the manger of black straw, the nubian madonna, the black star buttoning the white night sky.

N is for a white nightgown like a whispering simpleton, its sixty-six buttons are as neat as the exact pearly teeth of small boys. Unbutton button, he mutters, button unbutton.

O is not for seven, but for the 70 gallons of water needed to make the nylon of your blouse, the ruffles that are water, the small blue flowers and moony buttons sewn on to that water; fornicatrix, impresaria, executrix, ipsissima, mediatrix, in that blouse.

P is for how did that button get into my paté! We parade ourselves before the outraged gourmet, who counts up our buttons.

Q is for her query; do women have the Jungian Shadow? As many shadows as they have buttons, I retort.

R is for my retort, and for the gigantic retorts of the button-industry, who brew therein so much button-matter, which they puncture four-fold and six-fold, and distribute throughout the world.

S is for two knives crossed in the Shit, for the knife-fight in the dunghill which is the lungs of the farmyard, for the brightly button-eyed dung-flies that fume to the antagonists' sweat, for the steam that rises from the shit-dollies, like swift staircases stabbing swift staircases, for the calm snail deaf to aggression in the neighbouring cabbage-patch, the snail which is a cross between gemstone and dachshound, its phrygian cap of thin stone, its assertive towering eyes like watchful hat-buttons.

T is for the great button-shaped toadstools ticking away in the thunderstorm whose rain is the squadrons of silver buttons of a ghost-army marching down the slopes of mountains; is for the Throat dreaming in its silver blouse, the top button gone.

U is for Uncle whose glittering rings and smart
waistcoat buttons created Christmas phantasmagoria.
Look what I've found in your ear, Peter! he'd cry
out, and the hard fast hands darted to my head. It's
yours! he said, and it was never a stone or a button,
it was always a half-crown. His name was Bert, but
I remembered best his coins and his buttons.

V is for the V at the neck that haunts everywhere,
and is contrived by the loosening of buttons. It is the
nest of the squab throat, it is two-faced since it
reverses right and left off the pillared shaft and
gentle workings of the apple Adam ate. It plunges,
and my eyes slide down the long revers like an
expeditious skier.

W is for witches selling peppery sweets and emetics
in the little corner-shops: God-Stoppers, Coconut
Toadstools, Chocolate Idiots, Black Pontefract Cats,
Dagon-Babies and crackly brown Beelzebub-Buttons.

X is for the cross in the circle known both to Pre-
Columbian civilisations and to most of our buttons.
The dry mother buttons her blouse with a tearful
sigh: if a nipple is watching there's nothing to drink
and if an eye is giving suck it can't see. This is a
double-cross, big as two kisses.

Y is as bad as V which is to say better, since there are buttons running up the seam like souls sisterly as Pleiades ascending to heaven.

Z is the beginning of buttons. It is the flash of lightning from the moon that bites into the *pang* and the *ko* mussels so that they bear without help of the male. We lathe buttons from these shells that stand complete at her throat and play with the light like a rainbow tail-in-mouth at last.

Doll-Wedding

Bride and doll.
The hanged woman's portrait, ultimate vexation,
The death-necklace and the curse on the passer-by.
The smell pours from her like a ripped bag.
She dries to stringy toffee, the smell goes into
    autumn

The smell goes on the wind like an immense
Hanged woman's shadow cast across the world
She enters your lungs and hangs there
The autumn leaf cuts free
She hangs still in her icicle

By the time Spring comes we have forgotten her
She has however filled all the winds
Getting together with all the other dead people
Who share death out equally
With each breath, generously.

Who's Your Daddy?

(Ans.: 'H.M.S. Ark Royal!' – wartime joke)

I see a great battleship moored in the snow
I see the silvery pencils of guns that bristle
I remake this image, I try to,
It is a pine cone of lunar metal
Doors hinge in its steel, flakes fly,
Warm glows emerge
I see pollen
I see a pine cone consecrated to Attis
I see an ark
I know there are scrolls
Containing royal mysteries inside

Called explosives
Causing mysterious deaths understood by computer
It is a battleship
This will not be countermanded
It is a great battleship moored in the snow

It is not a white spider
Flying in its cracked web of the lake

It is not the discarded surplice
Of the summer-god, still warm inside

It is a battleship containing sailors
Trained to navigate and kill

It is no wedding-gown
Or wedding blouse with golden buttons
From which light shines across snowy sheets
It is no iced honey-cake of the sacrament of
    marriage
In which the honey is sweet light
That will last a couple of years
Of married breakfasts

It is a battleship

Commanded
Metal commanded
By a man with steel-ringed eyes
By a man with golden wedded cuffs
Under orders

It is no felled yule-log
Stuffed with presents
The honey-log of a sedated bear

It awaits orders understood by computer

It is the sledge made of dead men's nails,
The glittering horse of scythes,
The refrigerator of snowy carcases.

It's No Pain

Weather sensitive

I.
His bald head, the crystals in his bone
They creak as the crystals clash
In the snow-cloud. The genealogies
Of water are white and hung with stars
And crystal kings. They are
Glass libraries and jewel-shops
See the gale comes with his
Wide-barrelled gun and blows
The glass cases apart. Like a
House of windows or a glass cottage
All panes inscribed with the six-pointed
Letters of water, each letter
Different.
        This cloud
Aches the head, as though
The eye-whites showed banked snow
Within. There is a din
From the crystals rubbing
A great subsonic music like
An invisible hat large as a mountain
With the round brim of the horizon
Much too tight.

That flying mountain
The strange man wears its music like a hat
And greets me with eyes of snow-pain
His house warm as a dog's mouth

II.
He does not smile easily, not like a dog's mouth,
Full of snowy teeth,
His dog does that for him, the flies
Enjoying the warmth of his furnace
Smile grimly for him, their two pinions
Adjusted like the quirks of a grim smile

That snow-cloud is so black
That it could be full of flies
Half-dead with the cold,
Sub-sonic buzzing, the pupil
Of his eye in the white of snow
Black with his buzzing

Not his fault I feel the
Snow-cloud also, we together
Will pretend it is full
Of whiskey falling not
In flakes like a shattered
Glass but in spiritous tots
That burst on the lips

All that frozen whiskey

Going to waste on the mountains
But in the house it flows
All the whiskey

Dropped through the long winter
Numbs like the cold

His life freezes in it
I heard the half-dead
Buzzing deep in his gaze

III.
Then the snow drops and the whole
Country is one bright ice-flower;
The air is too clean and cold
To carry headaches or low sounds
Only those high and pure.
Within the millions of petals
Of this ice-flower we walk,
The blood in our faces
Like tulips and singing along
Our veins like millions of children
In red snow-clothes, and we know

The meaning of *millions*.

The millions outside answering
The millions inside calling

It was not pain, it was an *I am*
From the flying mountain
Great as us   small as us

IV.
The morning skiers ski by with their smiles
Dingied by the snowslopes, their mouths
Are furnaces of white smokes, they hiss by
With the noise of white snakes hidden in the snow;
All flows, except the water
Which no longer snakes in glittering brooks, the
    skiers
Do that with their laughing breaths while the water
Bears them up on crystal galleries. The mountain
    slopes
Are wrapped around with bitter snaking air, the
    flakes
Bright scales of the air-snake changing skins.

Of flowers of ice and letters of the snow, or
The ski-slope veined like a white moth-wing
Settled with its six legs on the mountain,
Water holding-fast and still
For our meditation - of course, we say, as the
    brook
Ripples in the sun like a concourse of skiers
Or rises with its breath into summery skies,
Water is six-sided, do you remember?

All the Skulls

The skull formed in bliss, judging by its grin,
True heaven packed with skulls, their ecstatic
   grinning,
So many skulls, like a snowstorm, all pure angels,
The blizzard of blessed fixity, with crystal teeth,
The great clouds white with their smiles, all
Light as white leaves, blown off the skull-tree,
What happiness to be light as a skull, and blown
By God's wind everywhere that blows a tune on you,
And shines a light in all of you, ranged over the
   sunset,
Singing; and the three-master singing as she sails,
The wind blowing through her tree-bones, and the
   light
Dazzling her canvas, which is flax-flower bones,
And the mountain singing from a larynx of slate and
   waterfalls,
And every little bubble in the mountain stream
A fragile skull of glass opening its mouth
To sing, and disappearing. The great moon
Floods over, like a birthday skull, shining

Miraculets

I.
The wind got into her cello and carried her away;
She was returned to us pregnant with Beethoven.

II.
He threw a lady's hand to the dog, he had
A great cellar full of bloody mucus in which
The memories of his secretive wives swam, he was
  defeated
By the youngest sister who dropped a jam-rag
  during the tango:
Cross-eyed and drawing himself up against the
  nervous laughter
'Yoni soit qui mal y pense' he uttered
And offered her garter and his hand to the lady
Who would not take either without the rest of him.

III.
He is fed on bread and water and tucked up
Into hazardous beds by old grandmothers
Who shine like ancient lanterns of horn and he
  always insists
On another story, another bedtime story
From the ghosts, he will have their stories before
  he sleeps among the ghosts.

IV. The tree of all seeds grew near the station, the
  two friends

94

Waiting for the 9.12 breakfasted on conference pears,
A girl waiting for the afternoon train to the shops
Nibbles at a palmful of loganberries, soft pink
    raspberries.

V.
Grave of a child accompanied by a bell beaker lying
In a sloping position so that the cup's lip
Touches the child's jaw buried five
Thousand years ago drinking his buttermilk.

VI.
Through the corridors of the bird's voices
I outface the butcher's blue eyes bullying as beef-fat.

VII.
A plough carved out of one great Cornish amethyst
The earth weaves past it as the planets weave in the
    waves,
The waves a broadcast from the skies, and the
    plough tuned to the centre.

VIII.
The spirit force in the roof of her mouth
Started squeaking and asking questions, the answers
Groaned in the rafters over our heads, all we could
    do
Was to sit still listening in her lamplit mouth.

IX.
The spider is a mere mask, it is
Brown and white ointments that weave her webs
With claws full of brown and white ointments, the
    same oils
That stream through the louvred chrysalis of the
Drab caterpillar devising fringed rainbows.

X.
Behind the strict dials of his electrical laboratory,
Behind its polished panels and its black and white
Indicators and scales eyelashing or goosestepping,
Behind its formal black and white like evening dress
And its dials like monocles
Rages the Spirit of Mercury in its bottle without air
Beating blue-silver pinions round the loose
    electrode, spiritus rector
Combing the fast pulse into straight locks of
    electricity.

XI.
The great wave-house of earth, breaking
Slowly enough to us, though we send
The wail up and up to do its work, long enough
For he and she to be parents, grandparents too and
    then
To dissolve in its walls and become its fractured
    spray.

XII.

A frog with sharp green teeth like thorns
Trumpeted like horns of green glass
Leapt from the bell of the flower and fastened itself
To the artery of his wrist, in thirty seconds or less
He was drained and the bed of lilies deep oxygen-red.

XIII.

The ship's screw reverses, a shudder
You can smell in the galley; I serve, however,
In the small first-class chapel where
The prayer-books are glass
And have handles.

XIV.
A bird settles on the ear of my portrait statue
Pecks at my eye blank as an egg
A small black bud breaks through my blank stare

In the small pool of rain that collects
At the centre of my outstretched stone hand
A rose-petal floats like the page of a sermon

I think I am beginning to preach

In the sun in the rain in the snow

Happily the little cracks laugh all over me

The last stonechips drop between the leaves
The statue's dust blows off the flowering bush

The bird's message from its hard beak

Three Aquarium Portraits
(Penzance)

I.
The lobster leans, and taps on the glass.
Among the fiery hands of light and ripple
It has a face like a barbershop of scissors
Shaving drowned men in a lambent steely light;
It has a face and shell
Of blue holly-leaves in a beating-gently breeze:
These details cleaning themselves always
Scissors through combs, and leaf rescrubbing leaf.

It walks like three headless armoured dancers
Of a machinetooled Masque of Industry
Who set their precision clawsteps down
With computered watery stilts on feathery ooze
That sends up gunpuffs. It sees
But it sees through sucked black stones on skinny
    telescopes.
Its swept-back aerials are the only red instruments.

It is *loppestre,* or spidery creature, but I dub it
Lob's Man, as a teamster gathers up his reins
Lobster has spikes and studs for harnessing to some
   evil,
Must be the jigsaw piece for some horn-hoof pattern
Being like a witch that marshlight blue
Carrying its hell's radio in those crimson aerials.
There! I can eat it with good conscience
Being our Lob-Star, the colour of Sirius,
Clanking on its platter, alive-boiled and buttered:
We shall eat the evil and make it our very own,
Cracking his male-claws with our silver pincers.

II.
This is one picture along the dark corridor
Of windows like a train under the sea.
Instead of scenery streaming, flocks of birds,
We have the fishes who swim their little masks
Of innocence with big dark eyes in silver faces,
Of pouting generalship, decorated fins,
And nibble at her fingers, through the glass.
With ripples, dusky lights, these frames
Seem full, as the passage is, with fiery hands
That push out with other portraits, as
CUTTLEFISH AMONG GLASS-SHRIMPS.

III.
The boots have golden eyes, like cats or sheep,
Slashed with a wavery iris, rippling welts.
They blush dark as fruitcake with a chewing beak
Deep in the centre of a flower of tendrils.
There is a creamy wand set in the moccasin
And when they slip upstairs as they like to do
Aiming this waterhose at their launching-pad
They are something between a pussy and a carnival-
    nose

Something between a fruitcake and a boot
A cross between a miniskirt and a pasty
Float water-gently like a gold-eyed turd
Of inscrutable wisdom among their glassy shrimps
High-stepping like lean assistants who are
Mainly spectacles and the joints of spectacles
Being entirely of glass with a few guts
But shining like a neon sign at every joint
Like ladders who are greenhouses and jobbing
    gardeners
Who are bees returning also, joints pollen-packed,
Easing their silver slivers like encased decisions
Of see-through steel whose clickering chimes
Bright-sparkle in water-sound, deafened by glass.

IV.

Among the always-twitching hands of fire
The creatures watch us, lobster
Ripped spiky from its pattern of imagined evil,
Precision prawns, those workers in glass,
And the biscuit-coloured, jet-propelled
And boot-faced cuttlefish.
They lean and tap the glass, and shiver
As we scratch back. To them
We are as they are, sea-creatures that float
With no support along the fiery corridors.
Through the glass
They wish to eat us, and turn us to themselves,
We lean back at them, our watery mouths
Like smashed aquaria with jagged fangs,
We return each others' looks among fiery hands.

Starwell

If the sky loses stars, this well is grateful for
    them.
If the sky misses stars, it knows where to find
    them.
Here comes the tall sky, to search in the well.
It will surely find its missing constellations.

You can't be serious! What, our lack be found
In water that trembles like a head of snakes,
That tastes of corpses and horsehair, sawdust and
    oranges?
Surely: the moon loves to slide through these
    corridors
Odorous as coffee-beans, and the sun has his
    counterpart underground,
She lights the well-shaft white as shells and
    trellises.

Perditus

(For Roy Lewis)

The cat looked through the brambles at me.
It smiled through the curving bines, a linear smile,
A powerful linear smile. The dew was dry.
My neighbour's dog waved to me as I left for work
The gulls were laughing like cats.
I notice many faces in the rocks this morning.
It is low tide. They are like buried heads.
No doubt the crabs are smiling with machine-tool
    faces.

A church appears on the hill where a grove was.
It stands on the smooth green with no graves.
It has a square tower with a dark door.
Tiny transepts. I lift binoculars:
The belfry springs at me, the bell inscribed
'I summon you,' it begins to sway
Silently, across the sunny gulf. The tower-door
    swings
Its rushy grain. Silently he walks out, his toes
Pace the drenched grass as if dew-drinking

I stare straight into his eyes across the broad inlet
I watch the strong lashes blink, then steady
Alight with friendship, surely I am hidden from it,
Raising a hand, staring straight into my lenses
    across half a mile,
Beckoning to me with a distance-shattering smile.

Perdita

The stigmata crawling
Like red spiders over the backs of her hands
The saint faints into my arms with a soft cry.
'Never refuse a fuck,' my doctor's words.
I unpeel her like a fruit of juice.

She sighs, 'What happened?' I say, 'You are no
   longer the saint.'
My prick rises like Jesus. One wound, in his head.
It is the Ganges issuing thence
In sacred wavelets.

Her smile is my laughter, my laughter her love.
The sun and the moon speed through our weeks,
   shining.
The red spider chuckles, hidden in some web.
A bonfire of black habits, golden shirts.

Pictures From a Japanese Printmaker

Exeter Museum, August 1974

I.

Actor robed for a bravura role
Caught in the rain. He lifts a fist,
He threatens the thundercloud
With slices of his sword. Lightning strikes
Like gongs. He discards his sword,
It lands in a puddle. He walks away from his damp
    clothes,
We are dwarfed by his erection.

II.

Actor in the role of a ghost-lady
Displaying a scroll. His high black
Eyebrows blocked on the white face
Hold, equilibrated like justice,
Sweetly questioning, 'Do you
Understand now, my dear?' before
She puts the scroll away
Tucking it into a sleeve
And rolls herself up.

III.

Women being carried across a river
On the backs of husky watermen;
Foaming robes, foaming water;
One woman glances down at the man's head
Stuck between her legs, taps the face

With her fan. The men are naked to the river
But for breech-cloths and head-bandages,
Their muscles tumesce against the dark brown
    water.
The ladies are particularly heavy, as they are
    dressed
In their own rivers of colour
Heavy with rain, heavy with river:
Each of the watermen shoulders his individual river.

IV.
Two girls on a country walk. One is a floating head.
She wears a robe of the exact greenness
Of the froggy pond they are passing, so her body
    goes,
Not even outlined, and her head is turned
Coiffured in oily valances secured with pigmy daggers
Like an armed head appearing above the pond,
Prophesying to her friend in blue.
One instant more:
The girlish friends resume their harmless stroll.

V.

A cave-shrine by the sea for communion
With the oysters the visitors sip from the shells
Fetched by naked priests who plunge from pumice
    rocks
Buoyant as waves-with-faces into the brine,
Pull themselves sitting on to the rocks,
Loosen the sinews of plucked oysters with their
    knives,
And pass them back up to the visitors for communion
With the sea and each other, for the silked
Visitors are drenched, all holy, all wet,
In the tang of oysters, holy salt water, and any
    pearls.

VI.

Samurai who gets his ki'ai shout
From mating cats, proceeds to contemplating
Frogs in order to improve his
Fighting stance, and his
Fighting expression, and his
Sudden leaps. Foreground
A trinity of frogs enjoy mud-experience
In a sickly cart-track. The Samurai
Is not yet ready for such dingy skills
Of camouflage, he is a
Clean fighter, in young fresh robes.

108

VII.

The story of the solitary house,
A gruesome episode, the pregnant girl
Hoist from the rafters by an ankle-rope
Over a small fire whose smoke rends to reveal
Her hopeless frowning face, while an old woman
Whets a knife, crouched by a block of black stone
    beneath.
The belly bulbed with baby lolls
So hard and fully-round on the chest
The breathing stops. We await
The amateur caesarian and the child leaping
Upright through the waterfall of blood
Straight to the withered tits and the haggard chest
That will cave to darkness in the monstrous lad's
    suck.
Out of this he will leap to beget himself
On the lady who hangs on her rope from the sky
Waiting for pain, the belly pulled round and tight
And taut and full and shining through the cloud-race.

VIII.

Beauties crossing by white steamer; the parakeets
Hackle-plunged in foaming cherry-flower; a Buddhist
    priest
Enraptured by butterflies that swoop in and out
Of his incense smoke, caresses like velvet cloth
The close-springing stubble of his vow-shaven head.

IX.
A hero in a faceless helmet, so fierce
His armour bristles with hero-light at every joint,
Confronts his enemy, a gigantic porcupine
Like a black sunburst prickly as he is
Whose face however has informed itself
With bright blue eyes, cat-slotted, and white teeth.
He confounds the beast by leaping on his sword
Balancing on its mirror edge to guide himself
Like twins of fire between the bestial prickles.

X.
Two women watch a thunderstorm
By the slid-open paper window, on the sill
A child pulls the pussy's tail, the women
Have a warm brazier of coals with bamboo handles
But the great cat of thunder strikes with lightning
    claws
And electricity pours from the mountains,
The dry light twitches inside the women. On a ledge
    above
Really enjoying the storm, in the pouring rain,
A liberated girl as fairy mandarin
Stands in the midst of flowers created,
Co-operating with electricity, by her feet
That walk surely among precipices
Storms and waterfalls no deeper than she is.

XI.

A ferry-boat's thirty-foot poles for punting
Across the deep river are gripped
Like martial instruments by naked boatmen
For samurai who ride the raft and fiercely gaze
Like wigged sunbursts everywhere. Most people
Avoid that gaze, as do the women
Hurrying across the bridge who tilt
Their great hats as to downpour and hide their faces
That way, with the brims. One, however,
Carries a hatless child who gazes frankly
Down from the trailing bridge deep into the fierce
    water-faces.

Aesculapian Notes

I.
On the domestic flight, the death-cloud
Bright as a silver ice-bucket in the early sun
Is an ice-vehicle, and just as the plane
Carries patterns of people within mineral wings
Driven by liquid rock: (all those hairs
And glinting spectacles, hand-bag clasps
And ticking watches, mineral carried by mineral,
The little administrative meat on mineral bones,
Gasping with jets, earth above earth,
Data rotated under stony dials,
The mountains echoing with us, round and round)-
So that cloud is six-sided flakes
Carried on wings of mist for water-purposes
With a little administrative air. Both plane and cloud
Are excellent in themselves, but death to each other.
Plane enters cloud, smashing the crystal galleries,
The stairs and water-portraits and the tinkling
Servants carrying clear goblets up those stairs
Which twine like escalating tendrils round that plane
Quenching the blusterjets and building one large
Four-armed flake that howls to the ground
Exploding on impact to smudged immense
    hieroglyphs
Uttered for miles across the even snow.
We think we know the purpose of our flight:

112

Now, respect and love that other flight of water.
I ride on the air-schedules, who rides on the
  snowflake?

II.
On the windy deck I spoke to the wind's clown.
That's thick hair slowly rises, that's baggy clothes
Swell with variable bosoms.
                            Now the wind turns
And she is sleeked by the breeze, like a seal
Plunged and shined by it, a lady
Groomed and streamlined by her weather.
                            Now the wind turns:
Half that's face is smiling against the wind
That's left sleeve flexes its airy biceps
That's good answers puff from that's fluttering lips
In patterns of air, pulsing passengers
Travelling by air to my understanding, and my hair
And clothes whirl in a carousel of air-creatures
Who pour from my mouth in queries as the wind
  turns.
These snaking creatures are our everyday words.

III.
Q: Is it something skinny that lives in the oak,
Something snakelike with breasts that gives the
    oracles?
Ans: Whatever enters the oak stands on every leaf at
    once
And speaks on tiptoe launching its passengers
Of wind on the wind, scattering oak-words,
Sound-shadows of the moving tree across to me;
Launching its light-words also on the shredding
    shadows.

IV.
From egg and wheat to serpent and horse:
Baking to music. It was the serpent in things
That taught us to squeeze and undulate the dough,
To loop it, slough it from itself, smash and roll it
    out,
And this is called 'bruising the serpent'. From this
    meat
We cut beige snakes and six-limbed men cod-pieced,
Pentangular girls and horses for them to ride
With manes like nests of serpents. Out of this meat
We cut a language to put back into the mouth
And for that instant before it becomes us again
We bake it brown and still. There on the flat tin
    trays

The breadfeast rests. Regarding it
The toothy gates of life are watering. Once inside
There are many journeys before it is stilled by the
oven again.

V.

Was it the wind outside, or the snakes inside?
The room had seemed empty when I laid down
I looked round the polished floors and the wooden
   walls
Before I snuffed the oil-lamp, but I needed my sleep
And the dream within it, and that confused my breath
With the wind in the oaks and the slither of serpents
Over the boards. Were there serpents there
In the dream-huts, as the stories rumoured?
Only with the light out. I woke once and immediately
The room was quiet, but I heard the slither begin
As soon as my breathing evened and that woke me
But this time I mastered my fear and laid asleep
Deliberately among the slithering, whatever came.
I woke to the bare wooden room made of oak.
I remembered how all the leaves had opened in it in
   the dark
And the dream was eating and drinking with wise men
   who were snakes
And who under the leaves had changed my body into
   their feast.
We had sliced meat off my sides, and with keen
   knives
Severed my joints that smoked in the cool night air,
My eyes were our staring delicacies, and my head
Our great crusty cake with deep torn sockets.

Now I am awake with a new body made of snake-food,
Having eaten their food I am adopted a snake.
We are passengers on each other, the cloud
Enters the plane, the plane the cloud
And the changes happen.

VI.
The cool air is heavy with its water
It becomes silver with its water as it touches the hill
The cold rock, and suddenly you see the stars
Of water are out in the sunlight
Glittering as they fall in their compendia.
The hill stocks up with water among the pines
In pure exactly-melting crystals, soon
Its flanks will stream with water effervescing with
    the heights
It has travelled and the new seeds threading.

VII.
The drunken oat-flies in the house-boards
Woken by their own hormone-orchestra and our
  furnace
Stagger out like old men on black ski-sticks,
They falter, they collapse, and the world
Is full of their shrill cries. Squashed flies
Indoors and pressed snowflakes outside,
A man listening intently to his hormone-recordings
And his winter furnace, that neat sporran
Full of warm porridge, meets a lady
In the midst of the crusty meadows of snow
Where they stand like two black ticks of a white dial,
They glide there with their ski-sticks.
My students lie abed, crushed into their fluey sheets,
They are full of germs, like squashed passengers;
This brilliant black boy is in ruxled linen
Like a fly stepped on by a white footprint.
I was crushed, I am myself again, my breath expands
In stairs and valances and hangs in galleries
Of white on white and through it fall the snow-stars,
The stars generate their glittering in this water.
A snowmobile slices hissing past the window,
The flickering window like a sheeted mirror,
The machine's track is like a crushed staircase,
Its smell like summer breath from lungs of metal.

A skydiver leaves his plane, builds downwards as he
  falls
A staircase of breath as tall as the cold sun.

VIII.
There is a little free-running spider.
It lives with us among the planks and crevices
And enjoys the furnace-air during the winter season.
It has the right, as much as we do.
It hangs on the ceiling, like an airstarfish.
It has the right of these winter oat-flies,
If it can outrun them, they are its harvest.
It will squeeze as many as it can, they are slow
Like hiccuped commas slowing the winter prose,
Like black plumes shaken from the nighttime winter-
    horses,
Their down-flecks float in bedside water-glasses,
They emerge hunched and concentrated from musty
    volumes,
Like museum-readers at closing-time. Though this
    spider
Looks extrovert as a barbed-wire laying-machine,
Even the spry lycosid is sluggish from the furnace.
It will squeeze many flies for its decent drink,
Tossing them aside like dry brown oranges.
The outside is a deep inside, frigid, unapproached,
The windows are mirrors sheeted by mirror-hands,
Swarming with glass animals, fractive and cracked,
Snow-paws loping slantwise, or plummeting
    straight
In steady pulses like glass skeletons,

In lovely resurrection-chandeliers soft as powder-
    puffs,
But however barbed they look, so full of clear juice!
They tumble into clear juice, losing themselves.
We shall live their deaths as this spirit streams
    from them
In brooks and peaty rivers and broad gleaming weeds.
During the winter of sheeted windows, this furnace-
    house
Is the world of metal lungs, dry hair, flaky oat-flies;
Now the sunshine at last turns these mirrors inside-
    out.

IX.

The real audience for my chalk-marks
Is behind, not in front of,. the blackboard.
I think of them like invisible black psychiatrists
Listening in darkened rooms to their fright-white
    patients;
Or as parachutists practising their craft of moonless
    nights,
Falling invisibly on black nylon drapes
Building the tall stair out of their long deep breaths
Tall as the cliff of their jump they take for practice.
I admire these earnest jumpers, these high lovers of
    earth.

They approach with whistling harness through the air,
Hands outstretched, steering their inevitable fall,
The parachute issuing like a syllable of power from
    the pack,
The great black sail thundering over his head,
And the lightly knee-bent running landing,
Child of the sky, born of an air-black precipice.

(Colgate University, Hamilton, New York, Winter
1974-5, and Cornwall.)

122

The Caterpillars and the Transformer (For Tomas Tranströmer)

In this window a telegraph pole of tight thickness
Colour and grain like spring water speeding over
  slate
Wires straight as the cords shoot through military
  backbones
A transformer like a top hat without a brim

A transformer, a transformer

The wind blows from the west and the wires glitter
  and shrill.

A lamp that at nights is a half-moon bracketed
To the pole that raises the transformer's hat

A transformer, a transformer

The nights lower the ceiling on us, with electrifying
  probity
This light on a pillar raises it to fourteen feet
Crowned with a transformer; in the white ceiling
The roosting birds squeeze long messages in tight
  claws,
Escape into the morning cloud-flow with its blue
  crackling gaze
Which either knows us or does not;
The cold clear winter rushes away under the trees

The caterpillars squad-march across the asphalt
They are like a big fat bank balance of spring moths.

Winter Oat-Flies

(Hamilton: Upstate New York)

Generations of black snowflakes, frail and durable,
Nothing to them, husk begat husk on husk,
A few jointed vestments put aside of a scorched
    colour,
Or walked by a dab of moisture:
Just bash the air near them,
That ruptures their skinny heart.
They fly with a soft hum, a low scream
And that sound is all they are
In a suit of dry fingernail, a life
Of tissue-paper and sliver, a lick of sun
Brings them out, or a fart, their instant
Resurrections almost hairless after so many
    returns
Like tan grapes or banded like oats. Winter
    sunshine
Shows labouring gizzards like X-ray shadows.
Lycosid spiders patrolling the picture-rails
Spare their leaps, it would be squeezing dry
    oranges.

I wish they had somewhere better
To hang their toy eggs like sallow bananas,
And unzip their coffins to a better life,
Some oak-grove for little Draculas...

The snow through the window has more strength
    than they:

Generations of whitefly-swarms rivetingly six-
    legged,
Glassy as myriads of cod-pieced gloss-suited
    astronauts
No bigger than these oat-flies
But pulsing down and settling in white cities
Like the million hands of the slow winter watches.

My Shirt of Small Checks

(My BBC Shirt - Ronnie Corbett)   To N.J.

I. THE LISTENER

And the radio said: 'I will be as a little sanctuary
unto them.'

It is a little sanctuary among the hills in the
desolation of winter.

Invisible rays tumble over the hills and through
the hills like a stiff breeze of watered silk that we
cannot see.

Minerals in the hills glow for an instant: Doris?
says Dan Archer, Doris? A whisper in the mine
galleries, Dan? are you there?

I believe that the madman can receive all these
rays in his head at one blort. His sanity depends on
the degree to which he can differentiate Cliff
Michelmore motoring over the wide sands from the
vultures of the nine o'clock news that have gathered
dispersing the macaws of Woman's Hour among the
doves of the previous night's Epilogue; meanwhile
the golden eagle of a budget broadcast flies slowly
and heavily into the full round setting sun of Desert
Island Discs. The madman stands under his
palmtree unable to switch off the birds or the sunset
or Cliff Michelmore. Oil from Wheelbase spreads
across the incoming tide like a supple breeze of
watered silk.

'Let Broadcasting House declare an amnesty and
a cease-fire,' cries the madman, as the Open

University flows over his head, 'for there is only noise where there should be silence'. My talent,' he cries, 'was to tune into the silence as I wished, to the sea, to the whale-song and dolphin sonar-talk (in which illumination counts for less than transparency'.); to the white crests of the sizzling ionosphere; to the moon as it flies overhead pulling babies out of mothers and dying persons out of their own gasping mouths, its strata bowing against strata, like an orchestra of violins; to the endless warm broadcasts of the sun that feed us all,' the madman says. 'Why, as the sun goes down, BBC2 rises, and passes across the heavens, and sometimes does not set until one o'clock the next morning.'

As for myself, I am no madman. My transistor is a block of singing minerals, and I wish their changes were visible to me, and as they gave me Uncle Vanya on Radio Four, I could watch the slow-blooming sparks through a transparent cabinet, the hour-glasses of transparent sands, the shifting spectra deep inside the instrument like the flashes of light off innumerable alert pince-nez, that turn into Chekhov's spoken words.

I regard this instrument as the hybrid of a choir and a mine, or something between a church and a factory, or the Houses of Parliament and the Research Division of ICI.

The cabinet-minister voices stride up and down its embassy stairs as I lie in the darkness visualising the salt woollen smell of their suits, the rain glittering on their taut umbrellas, the manly leather dispatch cases.

In the morning, a fly listens with me in the kitchen to Yesterday in Parliament. It returns again and again to the one spot on the transistor-cabinet, which I guess is transmitting information - perhaps a taste merely, or a sexual impulse - on a frequency beyond my capacity. I guess that this complex stone may have many different messages for the whole of the animal kingdom. I shall set it down in the midst of a rabbit-warren, I shall trawl it through the oyster-beds. The bacteria that alight on it and breed in the grease of my fingermarks pass through three generations during the course of Midweek Theatre, and who knows what powers of mutation A Book at Bedtime may possess.

My wireless drinks the sharp salt taste from the nipples of its batteries. As I replace the drained cells I pull a small curtain aside and gaze on the formal garden of coloured wires and soldered blobs, the sigil-scaffolding that strains music from all the other forces of the atmosphere, the musical intoxicant prepared from crushed air.

I am too gross to enter this garden until I have

eaten a small cake. Who in Broadcasting House
keeps a supply of these small cakes?

II. HIS FIRST BROADCAST
I remember how a certain old man who had never in
his life broadcast, died in this house, whistling all
its symphonies back over the air into his radio-set.
Now I sit in the kitchen, the fleece-white letter of
acceptance in front of me, glowing with its red
ranch-brand Twinbee Sea.

When I am broadcast, I shall be changed into a
complex vibration that is neither living nor dead. I
shall travel up and down the broad stairs of coloured
sands in company with the voices of prime-
ministers.

Whether you listen to me or not, I travel through
you and your apartments. Deep in the hills, the
mines speak. 'Redgrove,' they whisper, 'Peter? A
poem by Peter Redgrrrr...' and the beam wanders
growling.

For a mere twenty-five minutes or so a line of
black bats from Poetry Now perches on a white tree
of static. I am one of them.

George MacBeth has given me the small cake to
eat and I enter the garden of transistors and singing
mineral flowers. Now I should learn also how to
travel into the mirrors of every household, but for

this knowledge I shall have to go to the noiseless
dead poets, and to my friend who died mad from the
radio in his head and who daily scratches broadcasts
into my own mirror-skull.

Four Yogas

Yoga: sanskrit root *yuj,* to yoke, to link one thing to
another.

I. RAJA (The Royal Way: by mental control)

The chains wore out as he kept going, there was no
temptation to sleep.

The chains would not wear out if he slept, except
from his lazy tossing.

His clothes had been ground to flour by the chains
long long ago.

The journey was through an orchard that was always
in fruit.

When he was hungry or thirsty he reached for an
apple.

He had formed these procedures from the moment
they had shackled him.

It was always an autumn of apples so he could not
tell the years.

He loped tirelessly: the chains were thin and lacelike
after so many thousands of miles.

Their high chime had become shriller as their metal
had worn down.

A link snapped and a strand fell away from his left
shoulder,

Another caught on a root and like cloth-of-gold fell
away from his hip,

Under its weight the tracery tore like tough silk
never halting or staggering him.

He was free, and loped away under the apple trees.

II. BHAKTI (Union by love)
I sacrificed him in the chain-locker
As they weighed the anchor it was teeth on all sides
The bights earned their name, with the screeching
    of saws
Blood fell out of the ports flooding the tide
That bubbled with greedy fish-pouts. I had called up
The Iron Chancellor. I heard
A regal clanking like a linked regiment
Swinging their arms in a great assembly. I saw
Naked men and women swarming like white mites
In the mass of chain, the mashing corridors of his
    stride
And arcaded clangour. Some died in blood
Many also dropped in a trail like his lice
To couple, free links. I heard his martial steel
Clanking up the outside wall of the mosque, it stopped,
I looked up and met the gaze of two empty links the
    size of archways
Stained with blood like tearful wax and white clouds
    blowing through.
III. KARMA (Service)
She hangs the wet shirts up like large soft flies,
    linked.
A sudden frost out of the east. Upon the line, the
    shirts freeze.
'Look!.' she cries, carrying one in stiff as a
    chrysalis

Vast but very light, white-bosomed with frost.
'Listen!' she says softly, taking hold of a cuff,
Bending the arm, which creaks like a cello.

IV. JNANA (not this, not this)
tick and clank together like clocks
like linked moments, though
each link was a year curving
through summer to rusty autumn
to winter cold as iron

with iron clothes on

ladders with closed rungs
ladders into the soil.

I dared touch the sentences of the prisoners that
    issued from them
In cold links that were buried, the soil of England is
    full of these chains
Of shed blood, in linked sentences. As I dug in the
    kitchen garden
My spade clanged on them, I freed them with my
    trowel
Heavy with rust and clogged like the roots of a
    vanished tree.
See! the short sentences can be hauled out easily

Though some of these brief ones have exceptionally
    heavy links.
A long sentence is built like a necklace, to start with,
    the light links
And in the middle very heavy, though occasionally
    towards the middle
Slender links lay almost free from rust, denoting
    some bright friendship
In the closed world of prison. Towards the end time
    dragged again
And the links grew thicker. Some sentences, the
    never-ending ones,
Plunged deep in the soil and wrapped bones:
The life sentences, whose later links gripped the
    earth's centre.

The soil rich in iron favours dusky grapes
Which grow sweet against our mellow walls.
When the monastery had ceased to be a prison –
    there was no record!
I like to think the prisoners suddenly found they had
    always been free.
One day some lifer in his cell to scratch his nose
Moved his hand out of its gyve before he realised it
    was impossible,
To and fro out of its ring he moved his hand,
    disbelieving,

Laughing, then like stepping out of the cold metal
    reflection of a pierglass
One foot forward out of its gyve, back again, a
    sudden leap
Laughing at the empty husk riveted to the stone,
    through the door
(Never locked since the prisoners are chained) to
    the next cell

And shows his comrades there the simple trick,
They all leap from their chains, fall to their knees
Deciding to become monks, being accustomed to
    celibacy.

The late sun gilds their chains
Vacant like golden skeletons
Or like the ringed skins of dragon flies hanging on
    the walls
Scrawling the stone with their loopy shadows

Many cells crumbled, from others
They filed the irons free, hurtling them
From windows with musical explosions
Settling in the soil
Setting me my task. I leave them be
They shall become the iron in my grapes.

Though, those old people, they should not have
   tossed away their chains,
They might be needed one day, ready to step into
Like scribbled steel selves, like men in chiming
   armour.

A Clean Bill

I opened my eyes and saw that the Houses of
    Parliament were gone.
I left the bus queue immediately and leaned over
    Westminster Bridge.
By the side of an unpolluted Thames I saw risen a
    great noble building of horn.
Its walls were transparent and packed with summer-
    coloured ladders
And scintillating rods that hummed. A division-bell
    rang.

Down river came floating a party of men on a great
    raft
They were attacking the defenceless building with a
    mortar,
A puff of smoke and a hard flat bang from their craft
Was answered by a detonation and a plume
Of fire from one honey-coloured flank of the great
    chrysalis.

I understood that a vital race was being run. Could
The parliamentary chrysalis come to maturity before
    the floating men destroyed it?
I saw that its chitin was eroded after the explosion in
    a ragged door,
Inside, the ladders and pulsating red halls with
    chandeliers

Of brown cartilage flowed in currents of travelling
    committee-rooms
An ichor gathered and sealed the hole but
I saw that the shell had been starred in cracks
And a darkness was spreading behind the great
    segmental windows.
Is this death, or the firming before the armour splits?
I asked my companion and the lobby bell rang again

Out on to the river-terrace came a fair man with a
    long vibrating nose
I heard him haranguing the raft men with their
    abyssal punting poles
A police-launch advanced upriver and its small-
    calibre gun spoke once
The raft overturned with a chorus of high cries
The chrysalis of the Houses of Parliament cracked
    with a noise of thunder
And lightning from the wet wings of the being that
    struggled to its feet
Shouting 'Stop the killing stop it stop it' in a
    pulverising voice.
The bridge cracked and I fell forward into the waters
Swept away into the eastern seas my travels reversed
My institutions gone my eyes rolling down into the
    abyss.

Night of Her City

The solar system has changed: there is not enough
  faith.
Only one night in a thousand years knows stars, or
  moon.
It is called The Night of Her City.
One hundred years of prayers petition clear weather.
Nine hundred years of prayers give thanks.
Millions of people wait on the earth's plains.

The sun sinks among terrors of unlikelihoods,
The world dark as a cellar, as a camera.
One star appears, millions sigh, the moon appears,
  they sing
On one note, five billion people making one chord.
The rumoured constellations emerge, the masses of
  sky flowers.

No-one tells stories, no-one weeps
All watch the young leopards and the brave star-
  women of the skies,
The moon westers like sign language

Beneath our feet the sun travels
The stars travel towards the millions who have not
  seen
Now a slight breath across our plains which is the
  dawn wind

The moon slices herself with the edge
One star of the morning remains, we retire within
    doors
To write our scriptures for the starless unborn.

Laundon, City of the Moon

City of flocking blouses, of mountains
Honeycombed with ink, of inkweavers,
Of weavers of diamonds and gold, city
Of gloves that can crumble rock, city built
Of humming telephones, by detectives
With crystal pens, by printing-presses
Driven by the night-frost, by editors
With great stained dictionaries at their unsleeved
   elbows:

Over it all that snowy mountain that floats, the Moon
It must be as large as St Paul's
Over the enormous polished reservoirs

I draw a bath in London
I am plugged into all the silky water-circuits, the
   tides

Look! this moonlight has given St Paul a new skin
A lover-skin, he has needed one for a long time

St Bride steps forward with her wedding-cake on her
   head and marries him.

At the Surgery

Give me a specimen, I will boil it up.
The doctor's meander patterns of small sharp blows
  over the back.
His mad books on their asylum shelves.
Leave your hat in the lighted cupboard.
The turbulent nose-garden, with its salty flowers,
The accomplished gymnasts of the winter grate.
Give me your specimen. I will boil it up.

I kissed her hairy slippers.
I made a holywater ice-pencil.
I dipped the red egg in the slippery custard.
'Your shirt is drugged, doctor.'
'Give me a specimen. I will boil it up.'

Two of the Books

Gregory Treviles, Robyn.

G: My Bible has three thousand pages.

R: My Shakespeare four hundred only.

G: Four hundred white years.

R: The black bits are nourishing

G: I begin the journey when the books are closed.   5

R: Like the palace of death

G: or the sun

R: They have doors of knowledge on every side.

G: *Your* book of knowledge is your fine clothes.

R: No!   10
    I know my Shakespeare as well as you do.

G: I can shut my eyes and open the book anywhere
    And read it off eyes closed from the balance of
        pages
    Between my right and left hand, any edition.

R: Oh!   15
     I don't know it that well but I suffer a sea-
          change
     I read the Tragedies till I'm a skull suspended,
     A ghost with unconverted open jawbone hanging
     In a golden smoke of words

G: You smoke too much.   20

R: I read the Histories till I'm an old
     Abused Queen with Jeroboam sleeves

G: There's a case for the Virgin Queen as Author.

R: I read the Comedies and become quite Vir-gyn,
     A girl dressed as a man.   25

G: Pluck her doublet over her head
     And show the world what the bird did to its nest.

R: There are too many sacrificed voices hunting
          through these books.

G: Poor Rutland.

R: Davy Gamm, Esq.   30

G: There was a man dwelt by a churchyard,
   Mamillius.

R: Drenched ghosts, Cordelia,
   Desdemona, Gertrude, wailing choric Queens

G: Tamar, Rahab, Ruth, Bathsheba

R: Eden, the Wife and the Snake like a wave o' the
   sea. 35

G: A cathedral of a book

R: Cathedrals
   Dirty from much use and crowds passing, like
   a quay

G: As common as the way between St Albans
   and London

R: Tearing a poor whore's ruff not the only
   crime 40

G: We have drunk, and seen the spider

R: The Smiling Spiders
That straddle the wedding; the Marsh Spider
With flickering belly, up to its hocks

In Will o' the Wisp; the Thunder Spider:
His legs bestride the ocean, with a flash   45
He turns it all to one veined frost-leaf;
The Craning Spiders of the city, or those
  with long
Red eyes, like cathedrals on fire

G: Only my first spider was Shakespeare's.   50

R: Yes, worse luck. What's at the bottom of the
  cup?
He helps me love as I imagine spiders, drunk
  or sober, or the maggoty Amazon,
Or the surface of stars, or God's warm gloves,
  maybe by reading him
On something quite other.

G: Your Poetry-Bible helps you pray   55
To Old Gods. There are only three spiders
  in the Hebrew Bible
But plenty of serpents, most of them Moses'.

R: He's a Bible who's a friend! We're moving
  house

By river this afternoon. Shakespeare will be along
Reclining near the transistor on the buttoned cushions   60
Open at 'If music be the food...'

G: This Poetry-Bible also speaks to me.

R: Like a mirror with a wife in it?

G: I burned a killed friend. The chapel sent up
Forty-minute plumes. The parson   65
Bombinated with the Bible,
He was ashen. I could not cry.
I took Shakespeare's india-paper pages soft as ashes
Into the gardens: ''Tis not so deep as a well,
Nor so wide as a church door, but 'tis enough,   70
'Twill serve.' From Death bound in leather
My dead friend's voice spoke a dying joke,
Tears bursting from me wet the page, the grave, my smiles
And tears at once were like a better way,
A counter-fire.   75

R: Eigh?

G: A counter-crematorium
   Of snaky golden locks that flame amazement.
   The clinker glows like roses on triumphant
      brier
   He has turned the life-switch up almost full   80
   The clinker grows yellow, there are singing
      hives
   Building roofs of gold. Reach in dear friend
   Reach in, break off huge handfuls
   Of moist honeycomb that has never seen the
      sunlight,
   Bring me your clinker of heads, your dust
      of brains...   85

R: Talks like the Statue of Liberty

G: You must be my torchbearer.

R: Me? Oh, Proserpina!

G: He is younger than the Bible

R: And some say, luckier.   90

G: You can't swear on him in a magistrate's
      court.

R: You should be able to

G: The Bible is God's Shakespeare.

R: Shakespeare is God's Bible.

G: God is the Bible's Shakespeare.   95

R: Shakespeare is the Bible's God.
   I wish he was.

BOTH: OH I WISH HE WAS!

G: His book is Shakespeare's wife;
   And whiter skin of hers...   100

R: Ink breaking the silence.

G: I twist the book

R: You certainly do

G: The pages are stepped
            like white waves stopped   105

R: I step down them, out of my paper robes.

G: Dark Lady, you are black.

R: Why, as black as ink, but comely

G: Beauteous as ink; a good conclusion:
If this be magic, let it be an art   110
Lawful as eating.

R: She's found a whiteness that shall her
          blackness fit.
Do you read me Gregory?

G: So long as I can spit white.

NOTES TO 'TWO OF THE BOOKS'

Gregory Treviles and Robyn Treviles also appear in
The Terrors of Dr Treviles by Peter Redgrove and
Penelope Shuttle (Routledge & Kegan Paul, 1974).
Gregory is a poet and psychologist; Robyn a witch and
molecular biologist. They are lovers, and also
stepfather and stepdaughter. The poem was written
especially for the Shakespeare Birthday Celebrations
on the South Bank in 1974. The task it set me was to
celebrate Shakespeare with as many references as
possible, while keeping to the feasible limits of a

conversation between these two particular characters. Those who have made their acquaintance in *Treviles* will appreciate that the latter is the natural solution to the former problem.

l. 16   *Tempest* I. ii. 398.

l. 24   Vir-gyn: the wise gynander or deuter maid. Folk-etymology: Latin: *vir* (man); Greek: *gyne* (woman).

ll. 26-7   *As You Like It* IV. i. 214.

l. 29   *3 Henry 6* I. iii, and passim.

l. 30   *Henry 5* IV. viii. 110.

l. 31   *Winter's Tale* II. i. 27-9.

l. 32   Drenched ghosts: Ophelia; Caesar, Banquo drenched with blood.

l. 33   Wailing choric Queens. *Richard 3* IV. iv.

l. 34   Matthew 1. Four ancestresses of Jesus noted for liberated behaviour. (John Layard: 'The Incest Taboo and the Virgin Archetype', pp. 301-2, in *The Virgin Archetype:* Spring Publications 1972. Tamar: 2 Samuel 13; Rahab: Joshua 2 and 6; Ruth: Book of Ruth passim; Bathsheba: 2 Samuel 11-12, I Kings 1-2.

l. 35   Genesis 2-3; *Winter's Tale* IV. iii. 141.

l. 39   *2 Henry 4* II. ii. 184.

l. 40   *2 Henry 4* II. iv. 154-5.

l. 41   *Winter's Tale* II. i. 44.

l. 45   *Antony and Cleopatra* V. ii. 82.

l. 56   Three spiders: Job 8: 14; Proverbs 30: 28; Isaiah 59: 5.

Line references are to *The Oxford Shakespeare* ed. W.J. Craig and to the Authorised Version of the Bible.

The Return of Mlle Valdemar

She floats in like a statue in a cloud
Dressed as the murdered ghost of a wronged wife
She wears a long white shift with a penknife
Fastened over the heart. A river of crimson foil
Gutters glittering from the blade to the hem.

Cat-suited with crepe hair and cardboard horns
I request the next dance in my shoes painted like
    hooves.
A wan smile says, pointing to the hilted pearl,
My dress precludes dancing; I bow and retire
Crotch throbbing. There is cannabis in the punch.

My ghostly lady on a red plush sofa, flushed
I am pleased to see, with punch, much later.
I punctuate my compliments with draughts of wine,
She smiles sleepily at the flame, I protest
That never before have I met a mistress of life
Carrying such emblems of death. A cardboard mask
Of Chopin dangles from one hand. 'Remember to die'
Embroidered on a sleeve. The fire
Roars up the chimney, trying to escape.

Can it be, I gasp, grasping her cool hand
Pale as a fishbone, that your vitality
With no outlet, rising to a crest
Gathers to this white phantasmal idea
Like a spume? Any decent faun
Such as myself, will know the proper use
Of such vitality. Shall we dance?

153

At last she nods, half-rises,
Then sinks back simpering, her finger-nail
Tapping the ivory haft. Grinning I reach for it,
It pulls easily from her chest
There follows, as the frothy beer the bung
A flow of stinking blood like warm pitch
Which leaps out into the light blackening my hand,
My crotch. Some strikes the fender with a hiss.

It smells of dungeons. Some strikes my mouth,
My right eye, the white body of this vital lady
Withers, flutters like a surrendering flag
On the black staff that leaps between us

Her dress a white spume on a sea of blackness
A white muslin on a black sea. Corruption seeks
A short cut from dust to ballroom girl,
Stuffs itself inside a white dress, white hide,
Walks with a white mask, in fancy dress,
The blood-burns fester. They clamour to this day.

                              Gingerly
I gathered up the white shred of her skin
How shall I excuse to my host the sofa-mess?

154

The Tutorial

"The baraka seeps in, often despite you, rather than
being forced to wait upon the doorstep until your
'intellect' permits it to filter through in an
attenuated form."
Rafael Lefort: *The Teachers of Gurdjieff.*

No, not like a toad, but squat,
Compact, a broad man, fifty-five,
Black eyes snapping in a bullet head,
Jaw like a boot, rosebud mouth,
Great creaking throne, some Eisteddfod
Gave him his chair, his coffered ceiling
Raised by *léger de main,* in it
The sea-coal firelight beat.
'Can you give me advice, Sir,'
I asked, 'to a young writer, myself,
How, out of Magic, health
And good writing, and money,
If possible, may come?' He replied,
'I was willowy, and ginger-haired,
I advertised, a fat manual
Of instructions and a basket
With a sistrum, wand, sword and cup
Arrived; for my degree, headquarters,
Something was removed and something replaced
In my head, some gland;
I grew short and compact, and strong, Sir,

Look at that'.' The bird-cage at his elbow,
He turned, breathed on its bars,
With a screech of the bird they leaned and bent,
Clapped to, slicing the creature,
The leather desk-top spattered with bird-blood.
'That is a great feat,' said I
After a pause to steady my breathing,
'That indeed, but more pragmatical - is it all
As poetical, and stern?' His shadow
'Beat wings in the firelight, he replied:
Dust is plentiful, write your poem
On paper with a glass rod, words that will pull
Dust in great furry bundles off the shelves
Out of the mouseholes in a scurfy script.
If the words are right, they'll be embodied.
Then clear the page with a puff.' His breath
Shot like bullets over my shoulder; 'My own skill,
Sir, is not of that kind.' My sweat arose. 'Water,
   young man,
Requires skill, and conviction. A brittling room,
Worse than a gasfire left on all night, the signature
Writes itself in clear water-brambles, fat.
Your name in air, now, that is invisible,
But charge the room with UV light,
It draws out of the air to write your name
In violet letters like twilight. They are syrup-of-
   lightning:

A minute thunderstorm lies highly compressed
Over the page, wear breathing apparatus.'
He breathed in, I felt faint, and out:
I stood in a meadow of flowers;
The room reappeared, the fire listened.
'The last in the series is flame-script,
The blood of a woman is a god-fire,
Write with your prime tool, do not char the paper,
The flame will burn upright, on itself
Sipping, the poem will arrive wavering
In yellow grass-flames and bowing smoke.'
He was too heavy for our planet, he rose,
His feet printed the boards like marsh, I said:
'Your way is not mine, these are ink-magics,
Tell me paper-magic. You inscribe your signature,
I do not yet know my name.' 'Paper is an abyss,
The gland they gave me was called "scanning the
    atom",
Patterns of cellulose open in the white page
Like whiter galaxies linking arms, with the glitter-
    flash
Of occasional gamma-rays, and a sound rises
At first like radio static: it is the music,
A fugal sequence sung by a greater chorus
Than could be gathered from all mankind:
Patterns rise to the surface and sing of logic;
They plunge into the black depths and sing of love;

They haunt the trees first and then the pages;
We make our books of them, they sing our books.
Faithfully keep your shinyblack scriptures
On your breakfast table unopened
                              like a low-voiced broadcast
Its message will alter you more than
Daily readings at the top of your voice
With the top of your mind. We call it...'
'Reading by osmosis? Preposterous!.' 'Try it.'
The walls oozed spittle. 'It is why
The bible's sayings fit, wherever at random
You pluck it open. A flower sings too,
It sings a flower-song: but a book
Even a misunderstood one, uncomprehended, sings
A mankind song. The world
Is better for a book, though like a flower
It seeds unseen, unvalued...' 'How to achieve - '
' - these effects. The white
Paper must be marked with black, the black
Ink must be stained
With white paper. If you are a writer
You search the black for its whiteness, and on the
    white paper
You place your black mark. If you are a writer
Mark your page and it will open to you,
Place your mark on your page and listen, listen.'

He breathed out, and the meadow
Thickened the floor; in, and the firelight returned;
He breathed out: it was blue sky; in, and the ceiling
   returned.
He breathed, I could hear their language,
The sun with the grass, the fire with the ceiling,
Saying: We are Magic. Magic is life.

On Losing One's Black Dog

An expression meaning 'to reach the menopause'

I.
Thigh-deep in black ringlets,
Like a shepherdess at a black sheepshearing;
Like a carpentress in a very dark wood
Sawdust black as spent thunderstorms;
Like a miller's wife of black wheat
The stones choked with soot;
Like a fisherwoman trawling black water
Black shoals in the fiddling moonlight
Squaring with black nets the rounded water;
Like an accountant, knee-deep in black figures,
A good fat black bank balance in credit with
    grandchildren!
Tadpole of the moon, sculptress of the moon
Chipping the darkness off the white
Sliving the whiteness off the night

Throw down the full gouges and night-stained chisels!

Coughing black
Coughing black
Coughing black

The stained lazy smile of a virgin gathering
    blackberries.

II.
We opened the bungalow.
The sea-sound was stronger in the rooms than on
the beach.
Sand had quiffed through the seams of the veranda-
windows.
The stars were sewn thicker than salt through the
window
Cracked with one black star. A map of Ireland
Had dripped through the roof on to the counterpane
But it was dry. There was no tea in the tin caddy,
Quite bright and heartless with odorous specks.
There was a great hawk-moth in the lavatory pan.
Our bed was the gondola for black maths, and our
Breakfast-table never had brighter marmalade nor
browner toast.
Two ladies in a seaside bungalow, our dresses
Thundered round us in the manless sea-wind.
Her day-dress: the throat sonata in the rainbow
pavilion.
We kiss like hawk-moths.

III. EPHEBE
The beating of his heart
There was no translation

Eyes so round
The lad looked at me milkily

I had his confidence
In the dry street
Out came his secret

'The Battleship,' he said,
'We're going to see the Battleship'

As though a flower told me
Opened its deep pollens to me

He had teeth perfect and little as
Shirtbuttons, fresh and shining

He was about eight
Like a flower grown in milk

'The Battleship!' he said
So lively   supernatural
His soft thumbprint
Creeping among the canines

IV. CRY JELLIES AND WINE
Preparing jellies and wines in autumn
Sad wife alone
The rooms golden with late pollen

The neat beds turned down
The children smiling round corners
Sweet-toothed, sweet-headed
Her fruit, her blueberries on canes

The sad wife who would not listen
Boiling jellies, filtering wines in autumn
What shall she tell the children

They will not listen
They love jellies, russet jams

The sad wife in autumn
Her jellies and wines stolen
Stolen by love, stolen by children

The rooms golden with pollen

V. A VIBRANT WASP

A wasp hanging among the rose-bines:
Footballer wandering in an antique market;
Damask and ebony, mahogany thorns, greenglass
  rafters, veined parquets.

Again he struck the wasp with the sheets of paper and
Believes he kills it; the wasp
Clinging to the tendon of his ankle looked very
  sporting and official
In black and gold clinging by the tail the high-pitched
  pain
Was yellow streaked with black oaths

He could not find the wasp-body it had been sucked
Along his nerves
                   after the rage
There is a sore pain turning to lust

That afternoon a plucky infant was conceived
Full of an infant's rage and juices
He struck once, and conceived

He struck at the wasp once, his child
Ran in out of the garden, bawling like a plucky infant
Teased beyond endurance in a striped football jersey
  among gigantic cronies.

VI. THE STATUE OF HER REVERED BROTHER-
    IN-THE-BOAT
She catches the bloodless statue of her
Revered boatman-brother a ringing blow with
A mallet; the pure note vibrating
Through the gouged stone sustains
For three hours of morning reverie
During which time at this pitch
(Om) her petitions come to pass
Beyond her expectations, or anybody's:
                        gardens, walks,
 Silvery lads and encounters among the knotgardens,
Clavichords humming to the shrill-chanting beds
In the manor dark as horn. Too soon
The singing stone falls silent and it is not yet time
To strike the next blow. Now that she has seen
   everything
It is time to strike the last blow, now that she has
Nothing further to ask, it is time to plead
That the rigid statue may grant its greatest boon and
   walk
As her living and immortal brother among
All the beds and garden beds and wives and
   grandchildren
Proved by the magic of her singing jewel; but first
Before he can so walk she must strike some blow,
The ultimate blow, the blow to end all blows

To finish things one way or the other, that will either
Reduce the great icon to bloodless rubble or
Free her brother to return
                          rowing in
From the further shore: either
Make the wishing-stone alive in granting
The goal of bliss, or
                          shatter felicity, all.
                                    (This blow
Is struck only by the lunatic when the moon is
Full and directly overhead and the stony particles
Aligned like the cells of a yearning throat
Ready to sing, the birth-passage of man-song
Through a woman-throat)

In the beginning it was violence only and the shedding
   of blood
That started the gods singing.

VII. AT THE PEAK
The tables laid with snow
Spotless cold napery

Tense white snowmen
Seated on snowthrones
Knives of sharp water
Icepuddle platters

Iceflowers

Carving the snowgoose
Slices whiter than pages

The sun rises
The self-drinkers
Swoon under the table,

Glitter the mountain.
The rivers foam like beer-drinkers

Devising real flowers
And meat you can eat.

VIII. THE TUTORIAL
My anointing
Gathers him
I draw the shapes of him
He has yet to learn
Over his skin
He recognises them

Flowing from feet to head
Baptism

He is a stony river, he swims with his head on the
    river
The brown body

I draw wings in the oil along his back
He is a youthful messenger

I anoint his chest
He is one of the facetious learned folk
Silky
It is my learning

I tweak his nipple
The county thunders
White oil
Displaces my
Black mirror.

The Terrible Jesus

It is the terrible Jesus
He walks on water because he hates its touch
He hates his body to touch everything as water does
(As Orpheus sang from the river of his body)
The ulcers close as he passes by
This is because he rejects ulcers
Anything raw and open, anything underskin
He rejects it or covers it with a white robe
He fasted forty days as long as he could because he
     hated food
And hated those who gave him food
And put worlds of feeling into his mouth
Lucifer came and tempted him out of natural concern
For this grand fellow starving in the desert
But would he pass the world through him
Like anyone else? Not at all.
He came back from the tomb because death
Looked like hell to him which is another thing
He won't do, die, not like everyone else.
Nor sleep with the smooth ladies.
Instead he goes up to heaven and hopes
For less participation there in those empty spaces
But from there he calls down to us
And I know those cries are calls of agony since there
All the sweet astrology-stars pierce his skin
It is worse than earth-death that destiny starlight for
     those
That won't join in, hedgehog of light.

This is the terrible Jesus. There is another,
And none will give him a name. He takes care.
He lives all around. I breathe him. He breathes.
Like the air we breathe, he is free to us.

Headswop

'But I would have you know, that the head of every
man is Christ; and the head of the woman is the
man.'

St Paul.

I.
A black-whiskered husband
Bare-footed
In a white silky nightshirt.

II.
The mines in the cliff throwing up great briny spirals
    like souls escaping
Feathery fishbones sinter the granite vent;
The insuck hoovers mackerel-shoals; the coarse turf
Palpitates with silver vessels. They stink the
    peaceful walks.
Mine-mouths white-lipped with fishbone.

Then the mine chokes on a whale, and the cliff splits
    howling,
A cascade of rubies floods into the night tide.

III.
Waterfalls of milk   white columns seething down
   the mountains
Curds like white snakes shoal the whey rivers
London smells like a feeding baby
Cheesebergs on the high seas

Flashing grey on yellow with flocks that feed
The leeward cheesing-ship fires a booming volley
Birds grise the sky, screeching
Like winged tomcats
With bright spades the miners hurry to their berg-
   work
Slice off huge wedges for their sweating holds

A white cloud sails by most brilliantly
A light sleet of milk replenishes the berg's lochs,
Restoring its slopes, curdles. Milk-loving birds
Sip upwards at the blue sky-cow's radiant white tits.

IV.
Mary Reason seethes the snail-broth, never-married.
I have said what she sees in its smeary surface:
Visions of qualified plenty and cockaigne.
That was snail-doodling. Now her knuckles crack
Like xylophones, repeating 'to work, to work,'

And, like a cottage loaf,
She crumbles her husband.

V.
In a white silky nightshirt
Bare-footed
Scratchy with crumbs
A headless corpse.

VI.
Her talking kettle, the letters of the steam
White news;
The written question posted
Within the brain-hole of a grandskull
In what manner shall it answer?

You seethe it, it whistles.

She has a whistle: a bone
Covered with pizzle.
She gives it a warming first
In her important place
She can call them up now
Her hand is a small cedar-smelling
Workchest of bone tools.

VII.
The head severed
Boiled in pitch
Bolt-eyed
Lip-gape
Its breathless voice

Whistles

Mockery

'Xylocide, xylotome, xylomort'

Stretching on its neckbone
Out of the pot

Mockery

VIII.
Under the bench
Hunkered in shavings
That's not Joseph planing lintels'.
Not Mary painting doorways?
Below the bench
Among curly shavings
In the smell of cedar
Who whittles gallows?

174

IX.
This damnable head is bottled Jesus!

X.
The chaste kiss
Of a mother
Brushes
His forehead
Says:
'What's it like inside me?'

Answer

'Witchcraft, Mother.'

XI.
We are in the plenty beyond plenty
A star dripping with light the size of a cartwheel
Hangs over the bonfire. The blind boy holds
A white stick dusty with ashes.
Across his throat, snakes
A healing scar, across the bonfire
A complete world softly calls
'Marius?' Their eyes open.

Cold Northern Jesus

'Attis sacrificed his manhood to Cybele'.

The needles of the
pine-tree shiver as if
there were a spring
of water at the tree-tip,
and green water not breeze were
running down the trunk and along
the zig-zag branches
glossy with their butters:

the pollen in the cones
burns like yellow flames
in dark-lanterns whose shutters
are blown open, slats opened
by the warm wind, wet
and heavy with water.
Through the whole forest
in each tree burn
thousands of potent lanterns
whose light is seed
Attis will arrive here
from sun-bleached Persia
cooling as he comes
among the lanterns of these pines
that in dull weather shine
and shed their saviour pollen
that makes his cradle and on which
he will one day be pinned

radiant with cruel conundrums
down through the ages
of water and pine-needles;
cruelty towards gods
springs up like the forest.

Pictures from an Ecclesiastical Furnisher's

I.
The black and gold wasp
Grovels over the crucifix
Stings the hands
Stings the feet

Stings the side

Here is a woman hanged
In soapstone
Here is a sow crucified
Ephesian tits

Here's ecumenical!
Jesus one side
A jade Eve the other,
The blood from each mingles,
Carves serpent furrows.

II.
He is a hypnotist
He baptises with water
With water, with spirit

A drop of water
Sounds the skin-note
Then He magnetises passes

Compared to this
Your shop!
Your church!
It is a dolls' tea-party

III.
The Lord Jesus hangs everywhere
In each cross of the curtain's weave
In each cracked facet of each dust grain
In the rivers of sunlight
At the centre of each windowpane
Dying in every criss-cross course of bricks
Everywhere
Engraved on each fingernail
On each hair in procession
In each tear each swathe
Or spatter of jissom

Everywhere

Except in the moonlight.
His mother
Veils and unveils herself
With a weave of crossings
Nothing holds her
No pins no rockets
Certainly not Jesus

179

IV.

Vicar, I want to tell you about
That collar it is a white gate
Hard as iron but disguised as
Clothing. It prevents
The passage of your understanding
Down your neck. You are
Clownish: dressed like a man
Whose head hangs
One and a quarter inches suspended.
It is a trick! Let the heads roll!
Or be a clown with an immense
Collar deep as a well and the great
Green-tangled understanding rises
Snorting and dripping water
Like an elder god.

V.
The spider spun a web
To conceal to conceal
The sweet Lord Jesus

His enemies are everywhere

They are not on this page

He bursts his cocoon
Silk-sack sweet loveskin.

VI.
The old stone cross by Mylor Church
Grows a bunch of primroses at its tip
A deep hawthorn-scent draws from the stone
It is much older than the church
It was the statue of a penis greater than a man
It has been christianised, that is, crossed
Crossed out over-disguised which is to say

Lightly-disguised: the horizon is what he puts it into
The whole harbour estuary is what he puts it into.

VII.
The Mark. The Cross in the Circle.
The Celtic Cross. The Wires of the Marksman.

'I have 18 sons,' says General Amin
'I am a good Marksman.'

VIII.
The Shepherd whittles crucifixes.
The shavings open their eyes and walk
And Baa-baa, two-legged sheep.

IX.
'Stars above, stars below; know this, and be happy'.'
Hydrogen to helium; burning sunlight, slow H-Bomb.
My tree drinks the light, says Jesus the Joiner, with
   its leaves
Dove-tailing the sugars of this sweet apple
Carbon dioxide mortised to hydrogen
Red apple I pluck and devour and digest
The sweet fuel-sugars run through my blood

As I lift my hands on fire to heal you,
The hydrogen dislimns, says the child Jesus,
From these sugars and they melt to water

Warmth and water, the transactions of hydrogen,
The Bible of God of my Mother's arms,
The water-maker from the stars. Look'. I piss
I am the water-maker from the stars

Am I not, it is yellow as sunlight
I twine the sunlight through its beams or the
   starlight
My mother holding It and showing me how.

X.
I am called the Word, says Jesus,
Because my Mother lifted me out

Of all her blood and water and shit
Lifted me to her ear straightaway
Put me to her ear for my first words:
Star, water, blood, earth, rippling snake.

XI. Hic Est Enim Calix Sanguinis Mei
Eat the apple this way, she said to Jesus,
Stretching legs and arms wide like a
Five-pointed star; like this? asked Jesus,
Stretching arms and legs wide making a
Six-pointed star; no, she said, like this,
Presenting him his apple with the dusty calyx
Raised to his lips, she gripping
The stem in thumb and finger; Jesus took
A large red bite which blazed white
Across the fruit, and with the bright
Juices fizzing in the sweet flesh
And in his teeth where Jesus' juices
Rose to those juices, he saw where he had severed
A star like a five-pointed woman who had
Folded herself out of the ground,
And out of the air, deep
Through the tree's wood,
And expressed herself in every orchard fruit,
Star deep in every applewood staff
Beyond the wood-grain: in those starry depths
Persephone wrapped in cool apple-skin.

XII.
I was unable to speak a word through my vicars
Their collars choked me
It was their cross
Piers parsival pierce-through

Suddenly I grab his collar
The edge cuts my hand but I rip it off.
What is the Grail?
His head descends

What is the Grail, asks the Grail of the Grail?
You are the Grail, says the Grail to the Grail.

XIII.
This is not an iron poker it is a soft gristle
And this is not a hearth but her legs are wide open
    there is a chimney
I hit the logs in the fire or are they snakes with this
    so-called poker
My bones ring and my sparks swarm up the chimney
They are like stars I smash down pronouncing their
    names
That take form all in the shape of animals these
    constellations
They are all animals but one who is a gigantic
    gatekeeper
With a great penis the learned call a sword on a belt

I step outside on the lawn, all the constellations
Crumble and run into the one great star
Bull, fishes, crabs, monkeys, gatekeeper, the
    evolutionary series
Piled into a bonfire on my lawn that is time in one
    flash
Or squashed rainbow whose colours recite the bible
    to me
In the version which tells of God's spouse

I imagine the whole world can hear these stories
The sky remaining is an attentive silence carved in
    black
I am attentive silence which is the gate I hold open
To let this new traffic in

It moves through the silence like long-legged light
And the gate nips my poker

Then I come to myself I am sleeping with the
    gatekeeper's girl-friend
I hope he won't mind but he has allowed it from the
    beginning.

XIV.
The new populations come in on the great summer
   waves
Some are surfing on coffin-lids but all are naked
The water-caves open like fruit set thick with seeds
Which are men and women sitting down in rows
   inside each roller.
The choirs of the earth overturn the great creaking
   cemetery trees
The slim white bodies slip easily upwards through
   rough soil
As easily as salmon do through dark brown falls;
The wave bursts and the spray-flash is men and
   women

The kings and queens squirt through the green stems
Expand from the flowers' centre you cannot stop
   them

Here's another Fine Womb You've Got Me Into Staan, Oilly.

STAAN: Remember, please, how could I have
        breathed force without gills?
        When I got straight out of the sea I was
        called Dog or Dagon.
        I wear my horns with an air that are gills
        for thunderforce
        You are too quiet, Oilly. I breathe with my
        Laurels when the atmosphere's
        Critical

OILLY: Was it a dove through the ear or a seagull
        With herring-breath or my tubes rippling
        Horns like the masts that flame amazement,
        and
        Was it I that lay on my back belly-button
        Brimming with old port and the demon came
        sipping
        And sneezing and beyond the fancy the child
        sat up
        In my belly and said Blessed be, for thou
        art blessed beyond women.

STAAN: O Christ is that going to be one spoilt brat.

OILLY: Let's see what transpires, shall we?
        Do you like my great Mussulman trousers?

STAAN: So Lucifer stalked down to the pitchpits and
         wept
       With branched candelabra crown-blazing
         and Mussulman trousers
       Because of his lights his shadows attended
         him faithfully
       They conversed with luminosity they jostled
         it they ate it
       They went where the light-bearer sent them

OILLY: Wet dreams of lightning; result, an ovarian
         cyst?

STAAN: Beyond. Delivery.

OILLY: It fits

STAAN: Exactably. You are luminous. Your cunt's
         horns
       Branched into the black cloud of your
         thundering bod
       The Chinese rain came pouring, those
         fallopians drew down
       Out of the wet fire a bright child

OILLY: Mozart?

STAAN: And why not.

188

OILLY: Your horns cracked into the cerulean sky of
        my Giotto patio
        Your body bucked like bright lightning
        bellowing
        You are the angel that made my tubes beat
        By praising me and looking like them

STAAN: Call me Cuntface, my lips of annunciation
        My fallopians, those horns, gleaming in the
        donnerblitzen
        I am Wombbrain the Bellymirror

OILLY: My Hero. Your locks bristle.
        Are those snakes, or thorns?

STAAN: Displaced carmines, hear the Gabriels
        barking,
        I've a mouthful of Kensington Gore each
        month
        My period's late, Oilly, condraculate me.

OILLY: Bloody good.

STAAN: Then kiss me, hard and oily; kiss me,
      Mardi.
      The flames ran over her body like water
      They shrank and made a horned lanthorn of
      her belly
      I came out like a greased pig, midwife
      Salome almost dropped me,
      Heavenly light is weightless. So I put on
      weight immediately
      My Mam put me to her ear like a 'fat gold
      watch'
      Shook me hard to start me ticking
      Cried 'Staan, what goes on down there?'

OILLY: What did you say to me, Staan?

STAAN: I said: Witchcraft, Dam, that's what you've
      got down there
      Three white weeks and a cuntful of gore
      Mam, but milk me first.

OILLY: What did I do?

STAAN: Then you galactified me, tittering. Smock-
      skulled breech-first
      I was born with my milk-teeth in and
      speaking five languages
      And with horns where they fitted you, Oilly.

OILLY: Olé! What a gala! Sparkling lettuce!

STAAN: Stella maris but women have shut their
        faces

OILLY: Poor Devil

STAAN: Wombs like steel mirrors they'll not see
        through
        Bleeding like Jesus
        I stumble from such houses my candelabra
          blazing at every joint
        Solid light looking for a lady capable
        Some Moonhorn Wombwoman my face fits

OILLY: Some Wetdreamlady counting her cunt
        The country of good magic and gambling

STAAN: Good lunatic. It's moonshine.

OILLY: Of course. See you next month.
        I got this sun-tan from moonshine, Staan.

The Waterfall of Winter
(Project for Dave Westby)

The White Worm Falls   the White Lady Falls
The Albino Noise swoops over the bloodstone cliff

The sculptor is in love with these Falls
In love with this cliff like beefsteak, with these
Water-lianas and cold smokes smashed,
Or white monkeys chattering in the smoke,
Or as though the slim white dead danced sideways
    through the trees
On a crossing wind

The sculptor cuts a monument of Merlin in the
    bloodstone cliff,
He swings under the smoky eaves on his drumming
    scaffold,
Wet in his shining clothes, the white falls running
    with rock-blood,
He carves the face beardless with salient lips and
    brows
That catch the water white with foaming beard:

A white beard of cold smoke and a white-sleeved
    robe that is alive
Over a blood-red body -
                                    or the white shadow
    of a woman hovering
Which the red body casts -

                              or the white lady's body
    beating,
Which rock-red Merlin haunts...

The youthful sculptor plants along this fast brook
All the pharmacopoeia a wise man needs
Should a wise red man come

Blue tobacco, dock, stringent oxalis

Across the lake you may see the Falls flashing
Like red gold under white sail

He carves the bloodstone penis
It sets a cunt-current pouting in the smooth pour
In winter it freezes and no longer wavers like a
    woman's;
A man of blood curdles in the white wife of water;
A red man marbled deep in the frosty woman;
In spring-spate over the warm mere the shew of
    thunder and enlightenment.

To Those Who Cannot Catch the Disease

(For Stuart Wilson)
Let not thy right hand know what thy left hand doeth.

I.
And we kissed goodbye, and he went one way,
And I went down into the country famous for cheeses,
To its strong dark pear-beers, the pear-honey
So thin and exquisite, shining in its jar
With a pale tinge of blue.

It was not Utopia. There was a Virus.
A limp in the right leg, a shortening in the bones,
A self-digestion, a withering to a dew-claw
High in the groin.

Little pain once the balance was found:
The labyrinths hypertrophic, the great
Semi-circular canals deep in the head;
Perfectly easy to get about one-legged!
Why did I ever need two?

Then the right eye: visions of black lightning
Mining the green fields, and in the night-time
White lightning like star-weld crammed with
    starheads
Sparking, a glue

Sealing the lid shut on awakening each morning;
Sponging your poor eye, and your left orb
Watches its mate struggling down the drain
Like a dead spider dried in a cave
Withered on strings.

But the left eye! What rainbows of vision!
Every bird, he can see its chanting
Like sunlight from each beak
He watches TV without a set,
It flies in full colour across the land;
He sees love everywhere, it is a blue mist,
It is lightning, noiseless:

Thus the afflicted, the sinister cult.
I wanted the great meetings
Of one-legged folk with one shining eye,
Right arms pinned inside their tailcoats,
Chanting with intelligence, left eyes
Ablaze with new broadcasts.

II.
Disease? It was a religion!
And there was a Bird
With feathers of fire that stood raving revelation
Invisibly and silently on the wakeful left shoulder.

Many could not become diseased. They joined sadly,
Anxious to perform small tasks, very humbly;
They prepared themselves wistfully to bait the
    infection,
Adopting an eye-patch, a crutch in the armpit,
A coat with long tails to hide their right legs
Crooked up in a sling, and pinned to the shoulder
A stuffed parrot to stand for the Bird.

The diseased prayed bare-headed.
They had been reborn.
Right sides were placentas.
Real persons were left sides.
Naturally sinister fed on the dexter:
And they told how a new head had grown from their
    crown,
The child of their left and their right sides in
    another dimension
The one where God lived
Who had come at night
With a burred whisper lifted the head from the neck

Turned it somehow and put it back.
All healed by the morning.
They spoke of this
In a burr
With a vibrating left tonsil.

The undiseased without revelation wore black hats,
In tricorn, three-dimensional headhouses of the
    world:
One day would raise it to one who would point, shout
The head! the *other* head! and all would point
And he fling his hat away and stand bare-headed,
Leg shrinking, eye shrinking on its strings in its
    socket,
Diseased at last and walking one legged like God,
His friends all pointing, all laughing and pointing!

III.
I went down into the country with my sling,
My eyepatch and my three-cornered hat,
My crutch, blue tailcoat all buttoned with silver,
Eager for disease, keen for infection,
All swept and shrived, wooing defilement.

IV.
The ghost-town, deserted by Dexters.
In each bolted shop with the shutters up
The material of that trade still plies its trade.

On the shoemaker's bench, a fine left shoe
Cobbles itself out of leather shapes
Stands on a bench, polishes itself glassy,
Rests shining awhile in the falling dust,
Fillets its own nails out and lays itself flat
In the proper drawers, in tanned silence reposes,
Starts cobbling again.

They say if a Sinister is in need
He goes to such towns where the goods keep
    themselves
At the peak of perfecting, again and again.

Hens gobble their eggs, lay them afresh;
Ham runs squealing to the knife, heals itself;
Looms weave sinister suits, unweave them.

Dexters run the country: honeys, perries,
Pears, wheat, queenbees, asbestos.
Some wait a week, others a lifetime
For the Bird to take them, or the Virus to wither
    them,
Some cannot catch it. I

Expect there are jobs there. I shall plead for a job.

On Having No Head

At the entrance to a certain Witch Museum, standing in front of a world-globe, there is the figure of a witch in a tall black hat and black dress. The cement fondu in which her face and hands are moulded is coloured green. She is offering in her left hand, as Eve the Apple, a ball wound of red wool stabbed with a peacock's feather. Her face is ageless, intellectual, with pronounced nose and chin, and an air of terror clings to her. She stands at that point both like a blazon of heraldry recording honours, and a riddling guardian who is there to frighten in order that her message may be remembered even if it is not immediately understood. At first the atmosphere of fear she introduces clings to all the museum's exhibits and implements, until their use is realised, and the nature of the religion comprehended.

I.

All Diety in the acne psalms
Scrubbed hands, surplices like dry white flies
Then the scabbed face clears
On his first high note
On the second, the skin goes,
A death's head in a ruff,
On the third, a headless choirboy
Singing true from a small void full of music
His frill stains with rainbow,
His frock stains with rainbow;
The vicar pouts, shrieks,
Picks up his skirts and sprints.

II.

In the last moment of headedness
He raised his face singing and a moonbeam
Picked out the ancient crest on the barrel-beam;
Witch countercharged on triple mount
Crescents in orle
Mound with peacock in his pride affronty;
This riddle decapitated.

III.

I lie waiting for her, in the darkness,
Quite passive, long and low down,
Like a bathful of luminous milk
Whose surface ripples slightly.
I have a head swimming somewhere in that milk

IV.

The death's head moth scents his female
Over acres of meadow, through layers of glass;
The smell of love beats off the morning-shorn grass
Of sunday suburbs, aunt has the kids,
The white beds wait. I smell love
In the yellow spine-hole of the child's skull.
I clap it to my eye like a telescope,
I try it on my neck for size. It is rather small.
I watch my world through the dead boy's windows.

V.

Lady, your thing is like a tulip
Planted in softest soil
At this red time of the month
When you are your own mistress, mistress of
    visions
And no harassed hubby scratches his budget of scurf,
No squalling families pound at your red door.
This, a Fall? In stiff file, two by two,
The animals go in sad procession
Skull after skull
Ad ovum ex ovo
To this moment
Of your beautiful neck.

VI.
The moon goes dark, like a power-cut,
It is this moment that teaches us to use
The emptiness at the head of the neck;
We have a head for that neck,
Ideas pop into it, it slowly stands,
There is no population-rise.
I have no head for populace, my head is where
Uncaught still
The lustrous wolf swims the snowy reservoir.

VII.
I have a head that leers in a certain entry
The museum visitors shuffle by me, I am a riddle,
I am the world's globe and a statue in lumpy stucco
Introducing it by Eve-offering in my left hand
A ball of red wool stabbed with a peacock eye-
    feather.
This is my witchhead, chinnose crescent and tusky,
Green as fresh grass, I have bones of witch-martyrs
Cemented in me. As I shuffle past me
I offer the eye-apple and blazon my own reply:
'Cunt radiant with red clew debruised' without
    effrontery.

VIII.
Heat the skull red-hot and make
Cockle-bread of it, crisp as cuttle.
Break my skull-bread, drink white wine with me
Mouth singing, tail singing.

IX.
Open the tomb. The rainbow streams along the
    streets.
Peacock radiance parades the skull's voluminous
    vault.

X.
Wanton Indra, peppered with yonis,
Forgiven, his dark skin ablaze with eyes,
Head forgotten, swings in his fingers.

The Skin

(For Mike Smith)

A floating green palace: the public park;
Bolts of silk by day: by night bolts of lightning;
And the river easing its way.

The lament of the river-bed, the valances of the
   candle.

Shadows live in the sunshine, not at night!
The stars are enough for me, and the spring,
There was always a spring in the night cavern,
The clothes come off with a rustle of static,
She is in bed, and asleep

I stroke her wet

The perfume winds out of her

The sun rises and all the animals greet it
With their perfume

In the sunlit fields
A horse gently rests
His great nose on my shoulder
Contented by my silk suit.

The Meditation

He has exercises in meditation
The purpose is to see the zodiac within
He places the zodiac in his mouth
In his darkened mouth   first the sun rises
He happens to be facing north-east
It rises from behind his right upper canine
It is a glorious day   the sunshine fills his mouth
He calls out 'I love you!.' and means that
While it sets like broken bonfires
Behind his left tonsil   the moon
Rises quickly from behind that same tooth
And sets quickly, skimming after the sun
The stars emerge flowing serpentine
From that same dog-tooth in the east
Pivoting around that small bear
Set in his hard palate where it joins the soft
That gags if you touch it, high up in the left

The pole-star if it were a thin needle
Would pierce his left inner ear
Round which the whole sky revolves

It is noon, in January, and bright daylight
From the snow wheys the outside face
But inside his sealed mouth all the stars
Shine on in darkness: Cetus and Eridanus
Rise before Taurus, then at tea-time
Orion springs into his head
With hairy Sirius snapping red, blue, green.

We notice the boy's beard has begun to sprout
Like a star-map of thin light bristles,
Discovering the planetarium in the mouth
Broke his voice and made his balls drop
And his true stars act within him.

Orison of the Skin

This orison, however long it may be
And however deep the sleep after
Is never harmful to the health, on the contrary
We experience well-being from the dreaming very
   noticeably.
The cindered buttons and the tang
Of ozone on the air, and the scorched sawdust
I was assured were Shakespeare's pain-o
Misheard, it could be Mosthaven's piano
He improvised too well and the thunder
Took him out because it saw
It could do as well, transposing
Sharply to the key of lightning, but we below
Could not listen because of the echo...
That orison brought Beetosphere more
Than a headache. No, *Sir,* get a master
One who knows how to draw
A genuine circle, freehand, and can converse
With the dry-mouthed sheeted dead and the demons
Like spidermonkeys stuffing themselves
With *pattes d'araignée;* oh my dear
This orison of yours, sung, laughed,
Babbled like birdsong, this pillow-talk, this
'I'm dying, kill me harder,' this
'Gesumaria,' is health itself.

These Lovers

(Car smash: USA)

The dead man is bearded
The dead woman is bearded
The cohabitation of saints
Halo on the penis
Death around them like a magnetic field
The smell of beards
Why does death make itself so comical
The lady's scalp around her chin
The automobile like a smashed hair-glass
The white man like a barber's pole
Of blue suit-rags and gouges
They sleep so deeply on the road
The red-eyed, whooping cars
The tan, bepistoled police
Come to them, their magnetic field
And the white doors open on a lighted place.

The undertakers are stark-naked black
Full-grown women   the lovers
Are buried in coitu in a great
White clam-shell with a wavery edge
Like sculptured surf   they are buried
Within a sea under the earth

Somebody

Somebody rolls a great window open
There is a spatter of rain
A beetle parades the shiny stone
A jagged leaf scrapes a sigh
The swimming-pool brims with leaves
It should have a net
But the leaf falls and the ice darts
The drowned puppy appears to me
In a dream of sopping leaves
He brings in his mouth a green branch
The stars roll overhead
They draw an immense woman-figure
Her hands splayed out to steady the globe
She watches and glitters. Her breath is icy
I see her in all the waters, which veil themselves.

Demonstration
of the Two Mirrors

a mirror of steel and a mirror of water
the magicians crowd round
what trick will he do
with the water-mirror
he pisses a camera
which takes pictures of him
between the legs
he steps aside
invites a senior colleague
with a beard like white caddis
to reflect
astride in the piss-mirror, and contribute

the mirror of steel is thin foil
it is called 'dry lightning'
he hangs it up by its edge
it thunders and shakes the loose light
and the thoughts troop from it:
his death takes the oldest magician by the hand
she is a young lady in a ruffled blouse
her breath smells of cordite
the Spanish magician in the cape
is handed a book of poems he opens them
his name is on the title-page he hasn't written them
    yet
it kills him
even the owner of the mirror gets a present

it is a fresh roll of heavy duty foil
to hang in his temple
to hang on the four walls of his temple
so that the breezes of his religion become thunders
and the movements of their lips become lightning
dry lips speaking like thunder behind dry steel

Approach to the Mountain

The pig of the sea   the white pig
Truffles in the surf   it gleams
In the midnight   I find my way
By the white sheen of my clothes
The black companion has a white streamer
The penis-man is in his big white hat
Shining in the darkness   we all have hats
Heavy hats of water that shine in the darkness
And clear the way   he offers a fly
He offers a fly to the mountain
I say it is not enough you will not get
A grass-blade for the price of a fly
Nowadays   pay the mountain with your hat
And you will get a fountain always bubbling
One that will comfort mountain-folk for generations
Pay the mountain and it will turn
Your cheque into a deer or a mountain-climber
There are always deer if you pay
The mountain a deer's price
The fallen pine-needles make a fragrant latrine
The night-fountains create white ghosts in the cool
    air
The mountain grows rich   it owns the world
Will it not grow too proud to transact our business?

Three Establishment Poems

I. GOVERNOR   (For Michael Finn)

how is the situation governed?

by those governing flowers on the desk

where is the governor?

in the vase

I see two irises only
two periwinkles
a pouting rose
and here is a snot-sized snail
under this periwinkle

don't touch it!

and the vase is pink glass
rose-veined
with two jug-handles

yes that is the governor
he has been governor twenty years
of course we change him daily

who signs the papers?

the signature is in the flowers
the flowers are self-signed
the luminous documents sign themselves

II. SURVIVOR

The old survivor on the stone
Is the stone, he teaches stone,
He has inspected all the stones, and settles
On this stone   at nights his stone
Keeps him warm, on sunny days
He keeps it cool, he keeps
The classroom very cool, he polishes
His thin cool scaly glasses
With a dry handkerchief, the cloth
Squeaks with dryness on the glass
Petar at the Petroma

With his chalky nails
He scratches on the blackboard propositions;
On the blackboard which is a stone, he knows;
In the university which is a stone, he knows;
Not infinite salty maybe
Constellated on the night sky of I don't know

If the stone cap fits, wear it for ever

III. ULTIMATE PROFESSOR

It is a freshman dog   with his nose
He muddles about the course

It is fresh to him   by the nose he's led
To the Professor's maple, where today's text
Has been piddled by a graduate assistant.
Our freshman absorbs the knowledge, lifts a leg
Deposits his yellow answer: it is
The Dog's University of flaming autumn trees
Crimson, teak, beige and carmine, vermilion
Lemongreen and umber, greater in one misty furnace
And smashed vintage than you and I can nose
While we're still human   that dog's treatise is
    called
My Fragrant Saviour of the Tree: a urethral textbook
Made of wood and water like our books.
That dog will be a Professor one day, already has
    tenure.

Baby Department

Chairman of the Department of Satin Skins and
  Bubble-blowing
Professor of Soft Yellow Turd-Study and Prompt
  Defecation
Master of Scented Farts reading for Spoon-Feeding

The Dean of Acrimonious Sweetie-Wanting
The Vice-Chancellor of Bedwetting
Emeritus Professor of Pap and Boobies

Baby University Press spells BUP BUP BUP
Those who graduate from here are considered dead
  or grown-up

Amazing Perfume Offer

Dead Hitler's breath   it's everywhere
Like seagull-breath   the seagull took the afterbirth
The breath of afterbirth-eating gulls
The funeral chant of Barbarossa, his hordes
Chew cinnamon   breath of the forest fire
Where pine-resin glides and trees are glittering
    springs
Before they are puffs of branching smoke   the
    pulled tooth
Smell it   it is Buddha's tooth   on the pope's
    breath
Chivas Regal   and the scorched smell
Of Apollo's metal skin as like Lucifer
It re-enters burning   a ray of Sirius
Falling on a dew of Minnesota   the latex reek
Of the condom obstructing the Messiah's coming
The core of the earth, green hot olivine
We are scented from Saturn
The hellish brass breath of the peal of bells
Red-hot from chiming his Sunday, and as he bends
To kiss the black child's forehead
The quick sharp tang of Gerald Ford's
Shaving lotion   that child's forehead-smell
Like new-baked bread   fifty thousand
Miles of American roads in the brandy
Of a Silverstone tyre   and hexagram twenty-four
From the I Ching, *Recovery,* gives the stony smell

Of the silverstone mirror in the convalescent's hand
Who watches haggardness   as we watch *Solaris*
The plastic garden behind the TV screen exhales
Its scents of sawdust and ozone   behind
Its picture of our Queen, smells
Like a Prime Minister after exercise;

But it is the smells you do not know you smell
Like the Moon's closeness, its towering surface, the
   rising tides.

Tree of Swords

A shower of swords from the sword tree
        in autumn
Touch it and it divests itself
        like a falling army
You are cut to pieces
        chrysanthemums of the severed flesh
Or across the lake you see the flashing falls
        the copse of sword-trees
The swinging doors of a fencing-academy
        echoing from cliffs
Where they practise in breathing silence
        but for their sword-notes –
The unwary friend cut to pieces in blood
        the scream, the chiming clatter.
Never in restful graveyards
        but on old fields of battle
Never in quiet mortuary enclosures
        but hard by motorways
Feeding on the splash of collisions
        on the old blood, on the old arrows
The swords rising through the soil
        cleaning themselves
The blood's iron running in the sap
        and the blades clean as peeled roots
Flashing high on the tree
        playing with air and light
Mincing the rash forester
        in a glittering rush

Back to the rusty soil.
           The rain drips bloody from these leaves
And all the leaves make one note
           in the calm breeze:
Rough serpent-chime
           irrefragable hiss.

Current Affairs

The witch-trials begin. Joan Rook
Led into court backwards
To protect the judge against her eye.
The judge eyed her, and burnt her.

Today there is a sudden red stake and a smell of
    ashes
A shock-wave and a bass cry in a suitcase
And in a carrier-bag. A bomb is a swift fire
That reduces to ashes and a wind
That scatters the ashes. In the judge's car
Rides a marksman with a small pupil of steel,
The cornices are lined with eyes that bite,
The bomb touches her on the shoulder, elects her,
    the same Joan,
Says, 'You are today's witch. Burn.' She speaks
Some blood. Ashes of glass squeal in the station
    winds.

On the Mountain

She, about him.

The guide unlocks the wooden plank door
Marked 'volcano' we step through and look down
In the musty pumice-air at the round pear-orchard
In the extinct crater, we enter the musky leaves
And crabby trunks, you wonder what magic!
What could have brought us here! Exuberant
You tell some of the magic for banishing winter,
The green priest sweeping winter
Flu out of the house with his switch of alder-leaves
And flabby catkins, whistling through the house,
Leaping, twisting, singing, clicking with the tongue,
Whisking the flu-look from the bed and chairs,
I say, Defence! and, Celebration! you contradict, you
      speak
Of how the dead men leave portrayed
In coloured sands and pollens thrown
Upon the stream, as his picture forms he is
Bid goodbye, released upon the streams; you dance
Stiffly stamping how the fluid-dancing goddess brings
The flowers and food, the heavy bouquets and the
Goblets of curry, you inhale deeply and fall silent and
We stand in the fertile crater with
The hot ground under our feet, and the pears
Like drops of warm milt, and our book of knowledge
You say suddenly, is our warm skins, one work
Bound in two volumes, but I hush you and I say
Be still, but you reply, Tell me than! how
Ever else did we get to the centre here? Us!

Blind Autumn

My face is closed
Because I am afraid
My eyebeams cinder the walls
If I look down we shall be engulfed
The dusty walls will drift over
My glance drills a well to the horizon
The winds rush in
I dare not look for the moon-phase
I would slice it like cheese
The stars would pink out
As our beams crossed

You look at me, disappointed in my closed face

But with my eyes closed I can see all the smells of
    the town!
I walk through them as through a liana-forest
Chattering with monkey-smells which snatch at me
Roaring with frying tigers from the fishshop
And the oily sharks from the docks!
Up in the sky, there float jagged white smells,
You touch me, a smell of white lightning,
My face opens, tears I cannot explain
Wash it open.

I expect to blast your absence through you

I hear the bells across the harbour
I taste their red clanging iron, it gives me fortitude,
I have an iron skeleton, bright and musical,
I turn to you, you are bright steel, you are springs.

I look out of the transparent steel window
The garden is full of lathe-turnings, bright with
    grease,
There is a rusty rose on a green girder,
There is a clang in the sky and the furnace-doors
    open.

A Thaw

thin ice leaves the leaf
vexatious, pasting the grey ground
the winter serpents
atmospheric ice-scaled
annular tides of snow
neck-twisting, they are leaving us
the Australians can have them
our migrations return
on the swing of the globe
in my eyelids
there is a picture of some prune-faced
monkey-goddess trundling an egg
on the brink of a cloudscape
it is a blue-and-white egg of summer
it splashes in broad beams of yolk

we don't countenance blood in the summmer
all wars are winter wars
if there is blood the sawdust drinks it thirstily
and the crowd howls olé
the mud of Flanders is pasty
if there are summer corpses they are sprouting

like this daffodil stuffing open its earth-crack
with broad green blades, you'd think
under-earth was all green to the core, with yellow
    flames
with this as messenger

the ghosts are leaving for Australia also
if a few remain they are soft breezes
gripping the edges of the lake
and shaking it out like a gentle bed
shaking out a squadron of birds
creaking with gorgeous waxes into the hot summer

my surname will not be used in this future
the surname is the bad person
Redgrove crawls through the generations
Peter splits a chrysalis
out pours the contents of the rainbow-box

flowers crack the old bones in this garden
what is ice?

Music for Octopi

A whalebone orchestra.
An evening spent deep down staring at the skull.
Or, under the moonlight, the chromium waves,
The nickel-jacketed boulders.

Each one of these raftered
Waves is better for smell
For dividing nutrients
For zest and population
For greens and yellows
For shaking fists and toppling quickset
Than any drama
Than any church,
Better as a commode

Dreamily loosening bikini-knickers

I the squid will assist.
I am a dab hand at lace and knots.

In the Vermilion Cathedral

Your moon ties a dark
funnel of tides,
roads into the sea,
the fishponds heave
the sea bobs in, bobs out;

your doing.

I wish you would step out of the sea;
some signs about you, not too terrifying;
a kelp girdle, a spiracle in your chest;
walk arm in arm with me through the flooded
    highstreet.

Instead there are vibrations merely,
guest appearances,
a spiral corridor in the soapy water,
the great moon walking far out at sea.

I sit in church, it is abbreviated discourse.
Thou, He, Jesus Christ and the Choirboys,
The true presence, and a little cake like a moon,
The curtseying priest in his frock keeping you out.

Be the miracle that you are!
When I say 'grapes' the wineglasses fill
Goodblood and I drink to remember you
The sabbath apples choir as I walk by,
I sleep it off in the battling rams' field,
The grass is long, the rams tranquil.

If you know all my names and my lusts,
My monthly ransackings and my private games,
I assume you reject me, or you are in the wine:
Visit me in the wine, and visit everyone who drinks,
We lift our glasses and you come to us,
Millions of us and millions of you.

I want you to speak to me alone, please step out of
    the sea,
Crush the red bottle in your grip,
Touch me at the nape, at the brow,
Open the sea-door with a courteous gesture,
Use my hair for the tides.

Without a bottle, without a glass
I shall wait in this room small enough not to miss
    you.

The White Child
Shamming Death

I look out through the window
at the silent thicket
of tangled thorn-stems
my hair is cobwebs
my fangs have grown
they rivet my lips
I am silent as wood
or the glass pane in my chest
through which I watch
tangled thorns
there is a shower of rain
tiny lens drops
heart-shine and beat
I look into myself
the rain beats and shines there
I laugh and stand up
my nails rivet my fists
they have recoiled through my feet
I pluck them out
I bleed and laugh
I swing my riveted fist
glass shatters
jagged lightning!

the room is silent
the bleeding has stopped
here is a carcass
bearded and fanged
he is a heap of dust
on the heap of soft dust
a white child
makes warm water
begins to crawl
through the shattered glass
through the tangled stems
the crowned dust
is shamming death
the dust grins
one taloned hand reaches out of it
helps the white child
over the black sill.

Et Clamant SSSS

I dreamed oh I dreamed thus claimed the minister
The church tower grew tubercular
And coughed and ran its cracks all over the sky

My God! the moment they touched the earth
        they were animals!
                      Mosquitoes yet!
Along the church walks under the yews jig jig

I said to the minister:
There were three perpetual choirs of Britain: the
choir of Llan Iltud Vawr in Glamorganshire, the
choir of Ambrosius in Amesbury, and the choir of
Glastonbury. In each of these choirs there were
2,400 saints. That is there were a hundred for every
hour of the day and night in rotation.

All of whom were animals
        as soon as they touched the earth

Mercy! gnats with grins like salivating keyholes
That sing and tiptoe up to me
That come like suits of armour carved in glass
With squeaking glitter and reechy wax
And leave like whiskery sergeants coated red
Full-cheeked and salmon-fleshed. They suck
The pages dry and rustly, the minister said.

I am no help.
His supersonic bible flies open on the bureau,
    cursing.

The Wireless Cunt

She dresses. I doze on.

Her dress billows into galleries.
I see swimming camels, a turbaned head
Smiles and begins to utter, then is pigs
Truffling among the female folds. We have mixed our
    sands
Her dress is sand-dunes swallowing up her head,
It is clouds that farrow clouds, rise
Staggering, march on with smoking teeth.

I doze on in our bed. She makes watchful coffee.
A peal of thunder echoes in her cave, and dies,
The bedroom settles. The finger-ring waits.

I say stop making watchful coffee, come to bed,
But how can she stop
Radiating? Coffee is helpless.
Herds of buffalo that turn into men as they charge,
Dark firs that ripen, drop pears and apples, that
    mountain
Crams and clears its slopes, I see it plainly,
Four times a minute.

Those are gods on the move, I must accept it,
I doze on in our bed, watching as she changes,

Gods changing beneath her skirt
Gods with flowery faces donning bathing-dresses
Gods with pigs-teeth
Thunderpeals in my hollow teeth

I look past her, it spreads everywhere,
It emerges, struggling with a black cloak
From the mountain in the window

It is gods on the move

In my dozing mouth the stench of rotting trees,
The blue light they give off paints my lips,
Under their branches the god walks through
Quickly, his face yellow as butter.

After her, dozing in the bed,
Nothing rests. Some great mother walks over the
   sea in the sun,
She is burning among the yellow sopranos.
Hold still, hold still, the snails sleep underwater,
The fingernails are beaked and chatter like parrots.
Who's coming? Who's coming? To still her skirt?

He brings lamps, goblets of fire.

One Half
of Three Poems Twice

I. DAMAGED STATUE
He breaks his stone shirt open
with both hands
his chest is flat and his nipples tiny
to which the sculptor
has fixed
twin silver wires that spring
and settle in the palms
of the figure
which has invoked him, kneeling,
alas.

II. I love white sleeves
The warm arms in them
Are like warm sunlight in water
And the purposeful hands
You are the lake-lady
And the mermaid
Got up for a ball
You raise your sleeves
At the brow of the hill
And the white waves answer you
But what swords do your feet touch
What do your steps cost you?

III.

People getting at me
The fat jolly woman floury to the elbows
The sour thin woman dragging her footsteps
The salty bearded man who twinkles kindly
They wish to take over
Reflect from me
Only the quiet stream that bubbles in the hills
Or the hills themselves before the houses begin
Or the beach of stones (though that is where it all
    ends)
Make no demands and leave my colouring-pages
    quite blank

A Preaching-Cross
and a Cell Beside
a Fountain that Petrifies

No, no, the saint is not turning to stone!
His flesh is prayer-young, pink from the ice-waters.
He prays in his praying shirt, as he ought,
Come into the cell and see the runs
Of praying shirts turned to stone, discarded but
So truly prayed they ring like bells,
Like porcelain: this, with the lamp inside
Glows rosepink delicate as his salvation-cheeks.
Up to the neck in the river, at dawn each day!
The river flows through Frome, no filth survives:
I have seen them tilt the dustcart's load
And as it touched the water the garbage changed -
Tins turned to doves and beavers, grouts to grapes
That swelled and burst in the praying water
And travelled on as wine. Where it lapped their stone
That firmed to grandeur marble, pink as veins.
Yes, Sir; it's all pink here, with health.
Come, here's his walking-stick of plaited straw,
His carved bones called scrimshaw, his mazy
    candles:
The toys he played with in his nursery stages,
The chamber-pot of boyhood - what wasted faeces!
Now he river-shits in silver dolls
That climb out on the bank and form encampments
Singing tiny shivery hymns of chime all day.

Just opposite, if you screw your eyes up so,
You can see the famed escarpment, at the topmost
    right
A shadow of the dragon stamped in the slate cliff.
That's where he threw it, and it splashed.
They say it will return and turn the turds
To turds, the birds and beavers to garbage
Once again, and Frome on crumbling piles
Will sink into the river, much relieved.

A Sea Voyage or at Least a Change of Scene

His doctor's voice

I.
There are too many medicines
A sea voyage
The hold is full of clocks
Sometimes the end is too close by their time
Sometimes too distant.

II.
A change of scenery
These hills they are thriving homes
For many beasts, they are rainbow coloured
They have slippery shadows
Who is this looking?
One of the maggots
That inhabit his carcass
Has got into an empty socket
It sees shadows that are endlessly deep,
That are other worlds end-on.

III.

Take a capsule
This is a harmless capsule
It will start the river flowing
Between the two lobes of my brain
But doctor this is a great discovery!
Yes I take them all the time
(1) It will make you very calm
(2) It will make you one of us
(3) It will make you a doctor
(4) Pass it on

IV.

This lady offers me a fruit
Instead of medicine
She offers me a pomegranite
Because she is sometimes away
She offers me an apple
Because of its five-cornered star
She offers me a banana
For her personal reasons
And a belemnite or elf-shot
Also known as a thunderfruit which is her dildo
Two million years old
It is a little tongue of smooth black stone
I say we shall have this as a memento
Agreeing, she smiles.

Moonbeast in Sunshine

(Sudden slowworm at Totleigh)

Talonheaded with obsidian glances
He threw his tangles through the long grass
Showed me a way this side that
Stabbed his white snout into his misdirections
Switched through a yellow flower into secrecy
Dived through a flowerstem and was gone

The slowworm confused me and was gone
He looked this way and then that way
A yellow flower outstared me the grass empty

Moonlight streaking along choppy waters
The foil creases as the astronaut beckons;
This wizard pointed the wrong way and it beat me.

Cross between electricity and melting snow
Hybrid of a moonbeam and a waterfall
Son of a lizard and a white explosion
Glittering dewcloud pierced by rifle-fire
Child of a speedboat and its splitknot wake

I look this way that - I fall between your pauses,
    unravelling
Stairs I may not descend, not yet -
Who is the slow worm?

Maze-tracer ripping up your clews in one swift
    gesture
One swift backward strike so I no longer understand
No longer see the way, like a wound closing,
Like a sudden change of waveband

Quartz-sand pouring into mercury
Self-made torrent of metal milk.

The Wells

Thomas Hardy's father when he was dying called for
a glass of water from the well so that, tasting it, he
would know whether he was truly at home.

I.
My message darted between the talons
Of 20,000 birds between here and Gloucester;
Perching on the telephone wires, they looked down
With their dry beaks as beneath their claws
The wires crackled, and as it sped
From her to me, they flew up, and settled
All along the line, like a black
Telephone-wave with beady-eyed spray.
She said, 'Well, I don't love you, and haven't
For years,' and as she talked I watched the fly
Walking the window plying its bronze
Snowshoe of a tongue; 'I don't love you,'
And as she said that I swear I saw
The pug-nosed fly lift its leg and piss.
'Well,' she said, 'well, I don't...'
And I don't now care what she didn't,
That 'Well,' was the important word, the place
Where she was sending me, and descend I did
For nights into the Well Hotel, its satin sheets
Of silt, the granite pillows, the sharpwater tasting
   lonely
And tasting of place, the closest to home,

The deepest I could get. These women!
The power they have, the things they say!
My message darted between the talons.

II.
You might have thought that, thrown over
By the woman, I should have sought out God.
Well, I say, well, I did. No, you say,
I mean, seek out Christ, whose love does not
    consign...
You stop; you remember that He sends
At the last Judgement, men and lovely women too
To Hell, like a great toothed coping of flame,
And cool Well was all my woman sent me to.
Now I am up for the moment and can talk about it.
You see, I don't think that Jesus' thoughts are clean,
It's either fire or clean spitless song to him, no in
    between.
These are my thoughts from where I was thrown.

III.
Can He, in his white robes, walk on the mud?
The scalloped sisterly flanks, the female yeasty
    smell?
In that woman of mine there was a well
She didn't like, so she sent me down.
There was no evil, though she meant to be unkind.
I never liked Jesus in that white frock, and this
Was no hole for white styles; here, like camouflage
And merging with the ground, the look is khaki
Pronounced, correctly, cacky, since like a baby
I love the mud, the soft capacious shadow-thing,
The sisterly water-earth like night in day
Lying in estuaries under the sunshine
That smells of baking bread. Can He
In his white clothes, walk over human mud?

IV.
My thoughts that made God come were never clean;
And when He came to me, no priest could see Him.
That's garments were not white, that boy
Was a mud-dancer, more than the clean bright God
Loved water and earth. Then I saw Jesus
On the estuary it was, by the black Cornish mud.
I called out: 'Hey, Jesus! will our fertile earth
Bear you up, in your stiff cricketer's whites?'
Of course it didn't, and I ran out to rescue Him.

Our differences disappeared in the masked earth.
I found His halo sizzling in the muck. I picked it up,
Polished it on my filthy trousers, handed it over.
He took it, with a quick flip flung it
Yards over the mudbanks, and there, spinning, it
    sank
Sizzling out of sight, drilling me one of these wells
Of space and dankness in which I sit out of sight
At the earth's centre. When he smiled at me
With brilliant teeth under the earth, and then
Clasped me, I trembled, was He death?
Was I a skeleton, all leathery from the bog?
But He let me go, and showed me to the Well
Downward, where to wait, so still.
My thoughts that make God come are never clean.

V.
Before I found the Wells, I thought of them as death,
But they aren't, they are a kind of church,
In which the water rises through the earth
In tidal services, without advertisement.
I had a shelf.
It cost me nothing to curl up there,
And watch the water rising, smell the silt,
And feel: and feel
The well opening up in me like a cunt,
'The organ I was born without,' says Jesus.
Before I found this well, I thought of it as death.

VI.
I used, as a boy, to think of angels
With a faint thunder of wings settling tiptoe,
With a happy face giving me great glad tidings
I never quite could hear. When I asked
'When his balls dropped, did Jesus wank, like me?'
They stopped their noses at me, and shrank away,
Flew off in great fleeces, with their faces turned
   away.
This made me shrink into my well.
I used to think of angels often, as a boy.

VII.
I am not sure how clean their Church is, even in its
   own terms.
See how the crucifix-head of Christ in its varnished
   curls
Lolls always to his right, just as the child's head
   turns
Dextrously as it is born between spread legs
Through the upright slit of all life: thus Jesus
On the spread legs of the wooden Cross
Is sucked backwards into mater, which is the Well
His press-officers call Hell. I plunge
The Paschal candle into sister-water, at the Saxon
   font;
I watch my Saviour reappear within a shape like a
   cunt

Those columnists call 'mandorla', and yet the
    eternal matrix
Is supposed to be clean Jesus. They have it arsi
Versi: the Mothers are first, and out of them
Comes Jesus, who is us, since anything that stands
    up,
And talks about it, is a boy, since Mothers
Love to listen to how it feels
To have been down there, and born, and how it is
Not to be the thing itself, as they are, always were.
Faust stamped his foot, and sunk to them. Well!
Jesus flies with big eyes on Paul's sky-blue dome
Sucking its nourishment with golden wings
Within the rainbow-box, grown upon the ceiling.
All the priests I know try to stop Him landing.
I am not sure sure how sexless the Church is, in its
    own terms.

VIII.
God passes into the Cross, and there His balls drop,
And His voice breaks, unlike the fluting priests,
And out of the hollow tomb He bursts, the spunk
Exciting Him and filling His godly Wanger,
With good talk in every tongue pumping through His
    halo.
God passes into the Cross, and there His balls drop.

IX.

I have to admit again that all that I admire
Is not clean, as this deep well is not clean
With its fog-coloured stones and its shining silt
And moss bursting out of the stones; to rest there
Is like resting in the eyepiece of a telescope,
To see the stars shining in the circle
Even at twilight, slowly turning
And meditating, as they will. In this passage
I think the true gods travel, and if we lie together
Embracing in their path, then, when we come
The gods come running through every cell
And leave us shining in the darkness of the night's
   well.
Which, I admit, is what I really admire.

X.

What gods? What shining? Is it like this Moon
That rises among fir candles, with the waxen light?
Is it like this thin candle I light among these stones
That draws the cracks out like fluttering shadow-
   doors,
Like a tree with shadow-leafage turned inside-out?
Far below I see the water, like a moon.
Far above, I see the moon, like water
In a long well, and I am in a church
Sunk into a hill, a reverse spire. If you

Have shared my cool well, I have shared my feelings.
The candle dangles from its almond eye.
Its light is the longest exercise I've seen,
An exercise of return: those coal-forests
Drank up sunlight to grow tall, and the land heaved
And squeezed them into the wax I have lit now,
Solid light of a mandorla shape, fresh as the
    morning,
Fresh and waxy as a baby's cunt
(For where a candle is alight, there can be no sin,)
Fresh as the morning one hundred million years
    back,
For this candle slept in the earth like God in a well.
It is like a well reversed, a return from the afterlife,
The Devonian sunlight eating down its shaft,
And wells are earth, containing water and air,
While this is fire of earth, electrifying its air,
And when it burns, it seems always to have been
    there.
Indeed, fire is everywhere, and just as the Well
Shows the stars in daytime, so this candle
Makes fire visible. He sank like a stone into
    the hollow shaft,
Down through the cross grain, and returned
    like fire,
His apostles candle-burning and sputtering with
    tongues,

Their heads of knowledge alight like candle-flames.
This knowledge is always there, the heads
Merely make it visible.
These Gods. These shinings. These returnings like
    the Moon.

XI.
Why do I dwell on sunlight, as I walk up these spiral
    stairs
Cut inside the deep spire, up to the ground?
These forests drank both Moon and Sun to make
    themselves large,
And fattened with the Moon's phases. In this wood,
Sun with Moon made one flesh, and their child
    appled there.
Jesus suspected this, returned to wood to learn,
Which is made of earth and skyfire; I was sent
To water and earth, wellwards, now I light my way
Out of this water-mine with candles of earthfire, I
    make my way
Out of water and earth into the upper air, and come
    into
The air of fire and earth of a Church, at Easter.
The candles blaze, and in every flame I see Jesus
Returning out of His Mother, grown up at last,
Balls dropped, a Bull, ready to be a Father.
We have groaned over his rebirth for two thousand
    years,

'What rough beast?' Ans: the same guy, resurrected, with balls.
I walk up these spiral stairs into a candleflame.

XII.
I am out through the great timber doors.
At sea, a white yacht skimming like a wind-blown Jesus.
A fishing-boat glides in, because of its catch
Halo'ed with white seagulls like a burst pillow.
On the church masonry there have grown great trusses of blossom.
The sun shines: this world is feeding on starlight
The moon shines, with a different note,
Like realisation coming and going,
Like a necessary shadow passing
Candles grow according to moontime as well as suntime,
Petrol yaws the yacht, under the full moon like a spun halo,
Waxes polish the fruit; I drink the world,
It rushes in with great gulps,
I fill my deep well with sunlit air:
The earth is made of cool star, drinking starlight,
My foot passes the starmade threshold, through the great doors.

XIII.

The great lid throws its shadow into the well,
The water darkens, and the tides turn it to blood,
Someone slides the lid off its parapet,
And crescent light shines down into the earth
As deep as it will go, and they draw water,
Water which is pure and white.
From ground-level, I lean over the well-lip
Of this water, stone, light and air machine,
And am a shadow, on the shining disc below,
A shadow without a face, whose face is down below.
I will have to descend again to remember my place,
And walk the spiral stair, which I am glad to do,
I have often been there. The great Moon
Slides its shadow across the stair.

Dance the Putrefact

Scenario for a Masque
(For Pete Farr)
'As he lay on his back, stretched out on the ground,
with arms extended, he marked himself out with
stones - the shape of his body, head, legs, arms,
and everything. There you can see those rocks
today.'

> Old Man Creates - *The Hero with a*
> *Thousand Faces :* Joseph Campbell.

I.
'The Avenue of the Giants,' he said calmly. Meaning
the trees, introducing me to the Village. I have come
here because I have a dance. All here have come for
similar reasons. Here nobody pries or condemns.
Your dance is not mocked, since mockery distorts
the dance. Everybody here has been dance-blind,
and here some have recovered their sight.

II.
We were walking in the woods near the Falling Leaf
Tavern, with its cellars full of liquor made in
autumn. We had explored the avenue of great trees
tossing their heads, with the church at the far end
whose font was full of the surprising water. The
dance of dust over the surface of the holy water in
the font made visible the constant movement in the
consecrated water. We had seen above the village
the flat dancing-ground that had never been touched
by a shod foot. I removed my shoes and socks and
walked with my companion on to the hard flat ground
dustless and warm. From this platform we surveyed
the village. Tall columns of bonfire-smoke climbed
into the still air, spiralling and twining from the
villagers' gardens. We had descended and walked
along the tidal inlet towards the beaches. The tide
was low and we strolled by flat sheets of black mud,
watery earth, earthy water. Secretly in my mind I
hear the first steps of my dance. Warm fires glow
from the windows as we return in the twilight. We
pass a smouldering bonfire deep within which, as in
a cage, mice of fire still race.

III.
Smelling of new-baked bread and sawdust in the
early sun, glossy as chocolate, soft as drifted

flowers, the floor of my dance is prepared by the salt tide. I hear the great mud-drum. Its first beat ripples to the farthest shore. It is a liquid mattress, a slack trampoline, cradle and grave.

IV.
I am very strict, in order that I may be very grotesque. I am very strict, because I am very grotesque. My white shirt is without spot, its collar-lappets ironed smoothly back, a red scarf tucked in the opening. My trousers of an equivalent whiteness, demarcated by a broad dark belt. Like a cricketer I am white, like a morris dancer I carry a withy, a willow wand. I am a person of sheer whiteness save for a slice at the waist, standing at the brink of capacious black. With my feet bare I advance towards the soft black mirror.

V.
With the strokes of my withy and my bare footprints
I dance my reflection on the mud. The mud is firm
but quaking, soft as a strewing of dark flowers over
a firm beachsand. This is the way I dance my figure.
Leaning out over the mud, with my long withy-wand
I draw stretching out as far as I can two crescents,
their bulge towards me. They are the eyebrows.
With a cry I leap over them and land up to my ankles.
These prints are the socketed eyes. With a sliding
step I slive out the nose and stand working the
trench of the long mouth a pace away. With my wand
I enclose these features in a head. I pass on to the
throat and stroll out a left arm, a right arm - the
hands come later - with a second bound I am ankle
deep in two nipples, whose breasts I now scribe
from my vantage points. A third hop, legs clapped
together, gives me the navel, from which,
swivelling, I mark out chest-lines and transverse
rib-marks. Down the midriff I dance the long cunt,
I furrow, I delve, I dance its extent many times, it
splashes me, I am dark to my belt. I dance along
the waist and make a left leg, returning to the cunt.
I dance a right leg, returning to the cunt. I finish
off the arms with hands that grasp and spread the
cunt. I take a fourth leap, and am standing in the
feet of my creature. I face the sun over the sea, she

streams behind me like my shadow, the small clear
wavelets advance towards me over the tidal mud. I
turn, I pluck my feet out and stamp them down
facing my creature, my left foot in her right, her
left foot accepting my right. The sun behind me
from the east casts my shadow into her outlines and
she configures with this part of me. It is time to
give myself up to the dance.

VI.
I am down, and within her! I have vaulted into her
boundaries and I am as black as she is. I am buried
deep in her flesh. I pull her flesh off her in handfuls
and cover my skin in hers. I prance, cool and
nightladen with exterior cunt. The black bed before
me is rucked. The black woman-outline has risen
from it and I dance within her skin. I am the black
woman. I am petal-soft, and my surfaces are
rounded and shining. The bosom of my shirt is
heavy with mud. It hangs and flounces like large
breasts full of black milk. The black lady minces
sadly loverless over the mud, she smells of tar and
sunlight. Where is this white lover? She dances
sadly on her own. Soon her lover will return, but
her disappearance is the condition of his return.
She will enjoy the sunlight while she can. Soon her
ladyhood will pour like black blood through the

drains of his bathroom, she will fade like a shadow
in a shower of clear water.

VII.

Why do I return again and again to this same action?
Because it is my dance. No one here gives reasons
or asks questions. We are here in this village in
order to dance. His dance is all a person has. It is
his datum. But I, I cannot read my dance, and until
I can do so I am condemned to enact it, and am
imprisoned within it. I am dance-blind. There are
so many other dances I could join! But now the
season approaches in which all the dances are
joined into one, the time when all the people's
dances are performed together. For the first time
in my life I shall perform my dance among all the
others, with others watching. None will blame and
none will condemn, for each person has his dance.
This season approaches.

VIII.

That season arrived this morning with the blowing
of trumpets! Six men in Sunday black clothes wind
the silver trumpets. Six women in village white bow
the small dark violins. The music awoke me in my
great tavern bed. I gather up my dancing-clothes,
which have been cleaned and ironed for me without

comment. I dress quickly and carrying my wand I
clatter down the wooden stairs. Outside I join the
procession of people dancing to the music up the hill
to the smooth stamped platform. The Flora Dance
plays from the six loudspeakers on poles that line the
route. The sun shines. I hear the Flora Dance play
through the innumerable beaks of all the birds.

IX.
I am afraid. How can I dance my desire on this hard
earth? I have watched the others dance the dance of
their own lives, the dance they wished to read. The
music falls silent and they dance to the sound of
their own flesh. There is a lady presenter with a
forked twig who touches the heads of those who are
to dance. I have watched the man who dances the
tearing and devouring of human flesh; companions
are selected by the lady to dance the dismemberment
he wishes. They jerk and thrash on the dancing-
ground like farmyard carcasses; he stuffs his mouth
with the pink flesh greedily; the soaking of blood
into the ground is danced with wriggling fingers.
What if I were selected to dance this part by the
lady? Would I do the dance justice, imprisoned in
my own? I have watched three men dance the fuelling
of ovens with their fellow-dancers. I have watched
the old woman who dances the sewing of clothes over

and over. Certain partners dance their assemblage
into great costly garments as she stitches their
bodies together; at last she rends them and the
bodies scatter. She dances only with her rags. I
watch a great company of men and women who
dance a Parliament, and I watch the enacting of just
and unjust laws, I see the Parliament dance its
sinking into the ground, not a stone left on stone,
and a new assembly arises. I watch a household
dance the knocking together of a ship of great size
from the bodies of other dancers, from which they
exclude a certain company. However, certain
dancers dance animals, who are admitted, and the
remainder dance drowning, crying silently and
clinging to the ark's human timbers as it sails
without them. The lady presenter touches with her
twig the heads of those who are to dance drowning.
She does not touch my head with her invitation, even
for that.

X.

The lady passes among the dancers and signifies the
beginning or the end of their dances; she turns them
out of their courses with the touch of her twig. She
is dressed in spotless white, more plainly than a
bride, in a manner suitable for dancing. Her feet
are bare, her skirt is pleated, she is fair-haired.

She must be the chief dancer, since the others obey
her, and obey the language of her wand. Now as
chief dancer she begins to dance the flowers turning
to the sun and the tides turning to the moon, the
chief dance that lies within the others. She dances
alone, the men watch her from an inner ring that
surrounds the dancing-ground, she is watchful among
them for a partner. She touches certain of the men
with impatient strokes of her twig, and they join her
in the centre. The men line up in a row, crouching,
with their backs to her. The lady wanders behind
them, inspecting, pausing as if to choose, rejecting,
passing on, lingering on some detail of their dancing
clothes, touching lightly the brim of a hat, a frayed
cuff, the sailor-collar of a shirt, the bare nape of a
neck, a chain around the neck, seeking, passing
along the line, turning on her heel, returning.

XI.

She has chosen her dancer and they dance joy! There
is a sigh from all the company. She has stopped
behind one man. She has thrown her wand away from
her high over the heads of the spectators. She steps
close in to him from behind and crouching like him
rests her elbows on his shoulders, her wrists turned
to the front. Her thumb-joints lie with gentle
pressure on his temples and her fingers stretch out

263

to suppose horns on his head, eight-tined horns. He
is chosen as stag, and the lady will ride him, 'and
tempt him, and he will ride the lady. There is a
dance of riding and intercourse led by the lady and
the man. They dance on their heels to signify the
possession of hooves. There is charging and
division, there is stamping and calling, there is
rolling, there is slow beating with the feet until the
ground and the hills rumble and the hills to me
sitting in the shade, no member of the dance, the
hills begin to slide. There is conjunction and
division, there is breathing and sweat, there is the
thumping of bare feet, there is the occasional cry as
the dancers turn but no further song. There is a
serpentine dance that coils figures of eight between
the lady and her stag who stand making two centres
slowly turning to watch each other over the heads of
the winding people. I who have not been chosen
cower for fear lest I intercept the glance of one or
the other.

XII.
Now the procession reforms and to the sound of the
trumpets and violins which replace the body sounds
that were the only dancing-music, the villagers
descend to their houses. None of them looks at me.
I fall in at the tail of the winding procession when I

have seen that they wish to pass me by. The procession dances a slow step in triple time to the music. My feet drag along the grassy path. I expect the procession to disperse in the village square. I turn into my doorway but my arms are gripped. With serious faces the two hinder dancers force me to continue with them, for the column of dancing figures has not dispersed after all. As we approach the tidal mud-flats, the musicians fall silent again, and the only sound is the chafing of skin across earth.

XIII.
The tides have left my dancing-floor glossy and unmarked. The people assemble on the bank, they pass me forward, and sign to me that I must begin my dance. I lean forward and trace the first features of my shadow-figure. I bound off the bank and stamp eyes. My fear has gone. With lively steps I leap and prance until I stand in the feet of my completed figure, facing out to sea, the red sun at my back. I turn and pluck my feet out and stamp them down facing the throng. They are black figures on the red sunlight sending long shadows down into the mud. Suddenly one leaps out of the sun into the mud and stands thigh-deep in the thighs of my figure. She is in white. Her forked stick stays planted deep in the soft bank, a thrumming silhouette. She crouches and

draws herself knees to elbows into the trench of the black cunt. She rolls round deepening the hole and covering herself with black likeness. She flings her arms and legs wide inside the figure in a black star like a navel.

XIV.
I caper with my black lady in the mud. Both lovers are present at the same time, at last. I dance earth and water. The sun dances fire. It reddens the black mud. I am a seed in her red flesh, she pulls me out of the red mud, we are trees laden with red leaves, we are glistening red serpents slithering in the mud. We dance seamless blood-marble with our sour-sweet skins joined. We interchange our red shining skins by scooping and plastering. We fashion new and surprising organs and wear them proudly for a while and then dash them away. She grows a mud-baby under her flounced and clinging skirt, and I suckle our baby with red milk out of the bosom of my shirt. We bury our baby and we stamp until it dissolves, until its very memory dissolves, then we resurrect our child. I bury her and she buries me in our world bed and we make red love in the queasy bed until the ripples of our embrace reach the farthest shore. Who are these people who signal the end of our dance with silver trumpets, with small

dark violins tucked under the chins? We rise, and tear off our garments and trample them in the mud underfoot. We dance towards the crisp foam that dances towards us as the tide rises. My red lady enters the white foam, I enter, the trumpets sing from their silver throats all around us.

XV.

I run gasping from the foam. The people advance to meet me and to the sound of trumpets and violins clasp a garment about me to warm my body. I turn impatiently from them to where my lady should rise from the sea to join me. The sea is empty and the foam crisps gently in hollow waves. The people draw me sobbing and shivering away from the sea and its empty foam.

XVI.

This lady has ended in the sea, just like the lady I made for myself. This dance is no better than the other'. The dancers dry my tears and urge me with many gestures to join in their dance. Why should I dance with people who are no more than foam and mud and tears dancing on empty bones'. But as I dance loverless, I forget. Another lady steps into the circle and dances to help me remember.

XVII.

Our dance ended at the tavern door, we have climbed
the wooden stairs, this new lady and I, we have
bathed, and slept in the great bed, and we are
dressing each other. I button her blouse gently close
up to the neck so that the points of her collar make a
little A. I pass her pendant engraved with the A and
the V inside the O, over her fine dark hair. She
buttons my shirt but leaves it open so that my throat
is bare in a V. The sun and the moon circle without
end over and under our bed and our table. The rain
beats on the hard-packed dancing-ground, and beyond
it the sun sets into tango fire like a launching-pad.
The moon beats out her triple-time. The clouds draw
out of the waves and fall foaming, and shed their
peacock rainbows as they will. The moon is an
endless necklace of white ladies, red ladies, black
ladies always leaving, always returning. I fasten
her necklace loosely around her collar. The blood
beats time in our warm throats.